I've Never Been Happier!

Pedro Ballester Arenas

Jorge Boronat

INDEX

Foreword

Pedro Ballester died at the age of 21, but his life spoke volubly of a greatness beyond his years and of a life well lived. Diagnosed with an aggressive cancer while at university, he continued to live with an undiminished energy and concern for others that gave no hint to anyone of the constant pain, suffering and hardship he was bearing. His smile and cheerful welcome all spoke of a strength within and a beauty of spirit that were quite remarkable.

He was a man of great faith and great humility. To all who knew him he manifested an exceptional ability to love God and those in need. Concern over his own predicament was nothing in comparison to the concern he had for others especially his family and friends and those with whom he came into contact during his treatment. He suffered most of all for those who were suffering for him. However, he just got on with it. His faith and cheerful disposition would not allow him to crumple or be defeated. He knew in Whom he believed and to Whom he had entrusted his life no matter how challenging the circumstances.

Pedro's last days, marked by intense suffering, were also marked by great heroism and great humour. He would never allow others to seduce him to be sorry for himself. His simplicity, his smile, the brightness in his eyes, spoke of a depth of mystery within which the suffering he was enduring was clearly being transformed. Pedro knew that the Lord was no stranger to his suffering and so, together with Him, he offered it all up for the Pope and the Church.

Remembering him now, and recalling those final months, I am struck by one radiant fact more than by any other, and that's the freedom which he so clearly experienced in offering himself wholeheartedly to serve Christ to the end. One sign of that freedom was, of course, his amazing serenity. Before our eyes, Pedro, in and through Christ, had become a young man of immense stature.

20th December 2022

✝ Cardinal Arthur Roche

Introduction

A few weeks before he died, after three long years of treatment, chemotherapy, travel, spells in hospital, pain and suffering, Pedro was speaking with Tom, a 15-year-old boy who had decided to follow his vocation as a numerary in Opus Dei. Pedro asked him in a faint voice, *"Are you happy?"* *"Yes, I am,"* Tom replied. And with great frankness, he put the same question to Pedro: *"What about you?"*

Pedro smiled and said with conviction, *"I've never been happier."*

Three years earlier, a few months after joining Opus Dei, he had gone to hospital for a back pain that had worsened in the preceding months and was already becoming unbearable. It was during the Christmas holidays of 2014 that Pedro was diagnosed with bone cancer in his pelvis. Upon receiving the news, aware of his parents' sorrow, he told them: *"You have always taught me that Jesus shares his Cross with his friends. I already gave him my life when I said 'Yes' to my vocation."*

Pedro passed away on January 13, 2018, at the age of 21, leaving an indelible mark upon thousands of souls. At his funeral, concelebrated with more than 30 priests in a packed church, archbishop Arthur Roche explained:

Pedro *"has touched the lives of many – and most without him knowing it – through his patient, faith-filled, happy and loving endurance during these last three years of an illness, which he bore uncomplainingly and with considerable courage and which has been both a witness to the beauty of life at whatever stage or condition and a great example and encouragement to all who were close to him..."*

When Pedrito committed himself as a celibate lay member of Opus Dei, with that generosity which is so characteristic of youth, he could not have known how the Lord would call him to follow in His steps even to the sharing of His Cross and His Sacrifice for others. But we know, that as he rose each morning, even from his hospital bed when able, he kissed the ground and uttered the word of Michael the Archangel, serviam! – I will serve! And so he did, with great magnanimity, with patience and good humour."

When I was talking to him one day about the possibility that he might die young, Pedro told me, *"Sooner or later... so what? If we have given our life to God, we have also given Him our death, right? I am in the Hands of God. There's no better place to be."*

My literature teacher used to say that he could tell a book was good if, when he got to the end, he would have liked to have written it himself. It occurs to me that a life is good when, on seeing it end, you wish you had lived it. Books that are already written cannot be rewritten, at the risk of being sued for plagiarism. Imitating lives is not a crime, and no one can report you for copying. In fact, Jesus Himself invited His disciples to imitate Him. All the saints have tried to plagiarise the life of Christ and that is why their lives have been so beautiful.

But imitating the life of Christ also includes imitating his death. Whether it is cancer, a heart attack, an accident or dying in bed aged 100, the death of the Christian always takes place on mount Calvary.

Psalm 116 says: *"Pretiosa in conspectu Domini mors sanctorum eius"*. **Precious**, it literally says, *"Precious in the sight of the Lord is the death of his saints."* Those who witnessed Pedro's death saw it before their very eyes. It was a precious death. How God likes to see his children die this way! Dying the way He wants!

Those of us who were close to him in his last years could see how he matured spiritually to the point of becoming identified with the Will of God. It was not an easy road and he wasn't always flawless. At times the suffering made him depressed. At times he would get angry with others or he would find it especially difficult to spend time with particular individuals and would get discouraged by his and their limitations. Yet holiness does not consist in being perfect, but in not giving up the fight. And of that fight, there were many witnesses who give their testimony in this book.

Here you will find anecdotes and stories about Pedro compiled from testimonies and interviews of those who knew him, from the notes he left, messages he sent, entries in his diary and also from accounts written by some of those who lived with him. First and foremost his parents, Pedro and Esperanza, and his two brothers Carlos and Javier, without whose help collating the material would never have been possible. This book is a token of my gratitude to Pedro's family for having shared him with us. I would also like to thank those who shared their recollections with me, having lived with and accompanied Pedro during the course of his illness.

The book you are holding is not a historical chronicle but, rather, a collection of memories, ordered more by themes than by dates, although respecting, broadly speaking, the chronology of his life. It is a description of his struggles. The soul's battle for holiness is always an epic journey. Those of us who contemplated Pedro's battle witnessed victories and defeats, tears and smiles, frustrations and joys; we saw him get angry and rejoice; we saw him doubting and trusting, giving thanks and begging pardon... living and dying. To witness the odyssey of a soul that struggles, suffers and overcomes, is a privilege, a gift, a lesson; but also a responsibility.

Pedro died in the early hours of a Saturday, the day of our Mother the Virgin Mary. He died while those accompanying him were reciting the Hail Holy Queen. He breathed for the last time when he heard on the lips of those who loved him, *"Turn then, most gracious advocate, thine eyes of mercy towards us."*

And that is what Mary did with her son Pedro, as with her Son Jesus. She accompanied him to the end and took him in her arms afterwards.

She will multiply the effect of his life and death.

1. Early life

Although originally from Spain, Pedro's parents met in Manchester. A year after their marriage, Pedro was born there, on May 22, 1996, and was baptised when he was 3 days old. Almost a year later came his brother Carlos and two months before Pedro turned 3, Javier, his younger brother, arrived. The five of them lived in Didsbury, 6 miles from the middle of Manchester. For their holidays they would go to Spain to visit his mother's relations in Seville and his father's in Mallorca.

They used to pray as a family and start the day with the morning offering. From his childhood years, before going to bed, Pedro used to pray a prayer that served him as an examination of conscience:

"Father, hear my bedtime prayer: for everything I enjoy today, thank you; for help and kindness from other people, thank you; for anything I have done well, thank you; for anything I have done wrong, forgive me; for being hurtful to other people, forgive me and help me to be better tomorrow; now be with me while I sleep

so I can get up tomorrow, ready for anything as long you are by my side. Amen."

At the age of 8, he made his First Holy Communion and received the sacrament of Confirmation in his parish. Shortly afterwards the family moved from Didsbury to Harrogate – some 60 miles from Manchester.

Around that time, he began to write notes in a kind of diary, although they were loose notes in English. It is striking that, in writing about the events of the day, he addressed Jesus. On his first day at school, he wrote: *"On my first day I went to James party. I was excited. My friend James played with me. Jesus, I love you."*

On February 10, 2005, he writes: *"Today was the most special day of my life. Today got to be an altar servant. It went quite well and celebrated it in McDonald's. I also got burnt at home by the superglue and it really hurted."* Then he adds with total naivety: *"When I was in the garden I lost one of my arrows in a 9 metres tree. I was very sad and said, «There is never hope in life»."* However, he concludes again with a prayer: *"Jesus guide me to what is right"* and adds a drawing of the Mass.

He found the change of city hard to take, but soon he adapted and began to make new friends. His school marks were always very good. He was hardworking, helpful to others, and his teachers were delighted with him, as can be seen from his school reports. They often refer to his kindness and his permanent smile.

At the age of 8 Pedro became fond of fishing while on holiday in Mallorca, especially underwater fishing. He was an active child with many interests who enjoyed cricket, fencing, rowing and golf. He also liked to take care of animals, keeping fish, hamsters, and rabbits as pets. He even raised canaries for a while – he had a couple named Pepe and Pepa – and managed to sell the chicks to a pet shop. Pedro also tried breeding fish to earn some money, although this first financial venture was less successful than a sandal shop at the North Pole.

From early childhood he had been used to praying the rosary. At the end of his first day at his new secondary school, he was waiting outside in the street for his mother. When she was late in coming he got a little worried and his simple reaction was to turn to his heavenly Mother and start praying the rosary by himself.

As often happens at school, he also had his difficulties with other students. Shortly after joining the new school, one of his classmates began to make his life impossible. He would continually annoy him and make fun of him; sometimes he would take away his food and throw it in the dustbin. Pedro didn't say anything about it at home so as not to worry anyone. His parents did not realise he was having a bad time until his teacher told them that they were going to put Pedro in a different class because that *bully* kept having a go at him.

After 5 years in Harrogate, the family packed their bags again to change cities; this time to Huddersfield, an hour's drive from Manchester.

So, for the third time, Pedro had to leave behind many friends and start from scratch in a new school; but he adapted well. After three months, a school report informed his parents that Pedro had already made many friends and was getting top marks. Soon afterwards the school gave him a scholarship to reduce the fees thanks to his good marks.

Pedro's love was especially sensitive to the needs of each and every person. He was very much at ease both with people his own age and with those older or younger than him. In addition, as the older brother, he felt especially responsible for the behaviour of his younger brothers, keeping an eye on them and when necessary, correcting them affectionately but firmly. Because of his gentle personality, Carlos and Javier tended to obey him.

Good humour was a characteristic feature of his life. When at home he was the older brother. He explained to Carlos and Javi that God had chosen him to be the eldest and he must live up to that responsibility. Then he added jokingly that all he expected from them was obedience and docility. One of his prerogatives was to be in charge of the remote control when they watched television. Pedro proclaimed himself the *"King of the Remote"*. He also chose the front seat in the car or the best bed in their grandparents' summer house, appealing to his "birthright". He stopped joking about this when he was about 11 years old and started letting his brothers choose.

Another characteristic that everyone recognised in Pedro is that he reached out to them and was very considerate towards his friends. Pedro was especially sensitive to the needs and tastes of others. Sometimes he would go with a group of them to play bridge. One day someone asked him if he liked bridge. Pedro replied quite simply: *"Not much... But they do."*

Pedro did things that way: in silence. He realised that he could help, and without posting it on Instagram or TikTok, he helped discreetly in such a way that often even the interested party did not notice.

His family were friends with a couple who had an autistic son a little older than Pedro. They used to visit the Ballesters frequently because their boy felt comfortable with Pedro as he was very attentive to him, even arranging for him to be allowed to train with his cricket team on one occasion.

Pedro cared little about what people thought or said about him. Once he was invited to a birthday party attended by many boys and girls from his school. Shortly after arriving, several of them started smoking marijuana. Without a moment's hesitation, he called his mother and told her that the party was over for him and asked her to come and pick him up as soon as possible.

His brother noticed one day at school that Pedro had been left alone during break. When he commented on it at home, his parents asked Pedro why. He explained that there were some boys there talking about dirty things and that, since they did not want to change the subject, "*it was better to be alone than in bad company*".

However, his friends loved him. On one occasion they had gone on a school trip. Pedro was the only practising Catholic. When he explained to his teacher that he wanted to go to Mass on Sunday, he was told it wouldn't be easy. He would have to be accompanied by a teacher and with so few teachers, they could not spare one to go off and accompany just one pupil. Pedro wasn't put off by this and invited several of his friends. They were not Catholics, but they decided to attend Mass with Pedro just so he could go. In the end, seeing that they were now a sizeable group, the teacher had to accompany them.

He was also very attentive to those most in need. One day he met a man in the street who was attending a drug detox centre and Pedro started talking to him. During the conversation, he discovered that the guy liked tennis and they met several times to play.

Pedro discovered once that there was an eight-year-old boy in the neighbourhood who had no one to play with. Although the boy was several years younger, Pedro invited him to play at his house. After that, the boy came to the Ballesters' door quite often.

Pedrito had a great love for the armed forces. During his years in Huddersfield he told his family that he would like to be a naval officer. He signed up for the *Air Cadets*, an air force youth organization which offers camps and instruction for young people. In a short time he became number one in rifle shooting.

He also began climbing and was made captain of the tennis club. After school, a group of friends would regularly come back home for a snack and to spend some time together watching TV or playing video games. Several of them went to his house almost daily and felt so comfortable there that they would raid the fridge as if they were at home.

On one of those afternoons, when everyone was going home, one girl wanted to stay behind. When Pedro asked her what her plan was, she asked if she could stay there a little longer. Pedro told his mother about this and they stayed with her watching a documentary on animals. Later the girl explained that she felt uncomfortable getting home early because of certain family conflicts and she found it much more pleasant to be in Pedro's house.

From the age of 14, Pedro began going to formation circles in Greygarth, an Opus Dei centre in Manchester. He used to go with his brothers every Saturday. There he was able to study, enjoy the company of other teenagers and speak regularly with a priest. He would often spend time praying in the Greygarth oratory. He continued to pray the rosary with his family and served Mass on Sundays in his parish.

As well as going to the means of formation and doing his prayer in Greygarth, he also took part in volunteering work, giving classes to children from run-down areas to help them in their studies. On many occasions he invited his friends to lend a hand, explaining that they should share what they had with those who did not have as much; and that this was not so much money, as time, attention and affection.

2. In Mallorca

At the end of the 2010 school year, when Pedro had just turned 14, the family packed their bags for the fourth time. His father had found work in Mallorca, Spain and they intended to stay and settle there. However, the stay lasted only three months. At the end of that year the job offer which had been made to his father did not materialise and in January 2011 the family packed their bags once again and returned to Manchester.

Pedro never forgot those few months he spent in Mallorca. The family rented a flat in an apartment block next to Alfabia, an Opus Dei club. He made many friends at the club and at the Llaüt school. Being so close to the club, Pedro was able to go there every day to study, pray and take part in the means of formation that were given there. He began to go more often to frequent spiritual direction and grew in his prayer life. In a notebook he began to write down resolutions and ideas from his prayer: *"Treat Jesus as a friend. Take advantage of the school chapel. Be constant in prayer: have a daily appointment with God. Do not miss it."*

For the first time he had the opportunity to go to Mass on weekdays at school and also got used to regular confession. "*Be honest. To be in God's grace,*" he wrote in his diary, "*to get back up when you fall. St. Augustine was a great sinner and a great saint. Must get to confession a lot. Serious sins first.*"

At the beginning of the Novena to the Immaculate Conception, he wrote: "*Show your love for Our Lady. Pray a lot to her. Use the school chapel a lot.*" His prayer life was beginning to take off and it was asking him to be more generous with God: "*Be attentive to what the Lord asks of you.*"

Although Pedro had a great sense of humour and was often pulling people's legs, it was noticeable that he never humiliated anyone with his jokes. He seemed incapable of deceiving, lying or making a fool of anyone. When conversations veered towards the defects of others or jokes about their limitations or mistakes, Pedro would quickly and naturally change the subject.

One day Pedro decided to escape from school with some friends across a field. Laughing, they acted as if they were a special operations commando, crawling their way through the undergrowth. They can't have done it very well because a teacher caught them and told his parents. What most impressed the teacher was that Pedro did not make much of an effort to hide. When asked about it, Pedro replied that the most amusing part was "*to see the teacher's face when he caught them.*"

Pedro had such a good time during those short months that when his family had to return to Manchester, he found it particularly difficult. Although he loved England where he was born and grew up, after that stay in Mallorca he quite often expressed his intention to return to live in Spain when he was older.

In January 2011 he was back in school in England and after a few days of intense study, was up to speed with his classmates. He began to go to Greygarth again each week and kept up his daily prayer. His parents had taught him to be generous with God – a lesson that had been strengthened by his stay in Mallorca.

His familiarity with prayer and his effort to go to Holy Mass began to bring about a change in him. He realised that God had given him something He had not given to many. Pedro considered himself a lucky man. He saw that Jesus had chosen him especially, as one chooses a friend. As he told one of the club leaders, he realised that God had poured out on him graces that He had not given to many.

And that thought made him realise that, if God gave him what He had not given to many, He would also ask him for what He had not asked of many. He considered as exceptional gifts everything that God had given him in his life: his family, his friends, his life of prayer, his Christian formation, his condition as a Spaniard born and raised in England and even his brief stay in Mallorca where he learned so much...

He knew, and felt, that he was especially loved by God. And such Love always demands more. When God gives more, He asks for more. And when He asks for more... it's because He wants to give even more.

Pedro was 16 years old when he began to contemplate the possibility that God might be asking him to give Him his whole life. During that period, he consulted and talked to people who could enlighten him. On more than one occasion he told me of his doubts. He did not know if God was asking him to follow the vocation to marriage or to celibacy, either as a priest or as a numerary or associate of Opus Dei.

Vocation is always a personal discovery, a private matter between a soul and God. He spoke daily to God in his prayer and always expressed his readiness. He told God he was ready for anything. That if God asked him to be a priest, he would do that. That, if He asked him to be numerary or associate, he would do that. And, with a sense of humour, he told me:

"However, I also tell God that if He wants to follow my advice, I think I would be a great supernumerary."

God is a demanding Father. He never asks for more than we can give; but neither does He ask for less. Pedro once remarked, "*I know I have that natural inclination to start a family because I'm a normal guy and I have a young heart.*" He understood that well. As he also understood that to give God one's whole life, renouncing one's plans, is always a great sacrifice.

One day, talking to the director of Greygarth, he asked him how one asked for admission to Opus Dei. Xavier explained that it was simply a matter of expressing his intention to the prelate of Opus Dei in a letter. Pedro said he wanted to do it and asked for pen and paper. Some twenty minutes later, when Xavier entered the room again, he found Pedro surrounded by a mountain of screwed up paper balls, his various "*attempts*". The poor fellow was getting more and more nervous as he wrote and discarded several versions of the letter. Finally, he got up and said that he would write that letter another day, when he knew what he wanted to write.

A little later, on May 1, 2013, a few weeks before his 17th birthday, he sat in the same office again to write the letter. Certain now that God was asking him to do so, and having prepared the content of that letter better, he told the prelate his decision to give himself to God as a numerary of Opus Dei.

Pedro had talked to his parents about his vocation many times. That day he had told them what he was going to do and when he wrote the letter, he told his parents immediately. Then he began to think about how to explain it to his brothers.

A few days later, Pedro decided to explain it to his brother Carlos. He told him he needed to tell him something. Carlos himself tells the story: *"When he said he wanted to talk to me, I smiled. I had noticed something wrong with him. Following a joke from the movie Mulan, when we referred to a romantic relationship, we jokingly called it a «**Mushu.**» As I had seen Pedro being very happy lately, I came to the conclusion that there was **Mushu**, in between. And when he told me he wanted to tell me something, I was convinced that he had fallen in love... and it turns out I was right! He had fallen in love... with God and told me that he had decided to give Him his life as a numerary of Opus Dei. When he finished I asked him:*

*"So... there is no **Mushu**?"*

*"There will never be **Mushu**, I'm afraid,"* Pedro confirmed with a laugh.

3. Trying out his vocation

From the moment he asked for admission to Opus Dei, his faithfulness to his vocation was a priority. Pedro was a handsome and brilliant boy who did not pass unnoticed.

One day, a girl in his Confirmation class asked him to go out for a walk. Pedro wanted to nip any potential romantic interest in the bud and thought about how to explain to her quickly that he had no intention of dating girls. He told her quite bluntly, "*I have given my life to God.*"

The poor girl was very surprised by that answer, but she immediately recovered and replied: "*I knew it was too good to be true!*"

Once they were visited by their grandparents. Pedro is the name of his father, grandfather and great-grandfather. To avoid confusion, Pedro Junior was called Pedrito. Commenting on the family tradition of passing on Pedro's name from generation to generation, Pedrito commented with a smile: "*The tradition ends here.*"

In a conversation with one of the older numeraries, Pedro was asked how he was getting on with his vocation. It had come out in the discussion that many young people found it difficult to be faithful to their path. Pedro wanted to clarify any doubts about his intention to remain faithful and told him with a smile:

"Don't worry. I'm here for the long haul."

With his newly inaugurated vocation, Pedro saw himself as the apostle John. One day he wrote in his prayer: *"It's funny how, of the apostles, only John was left to accompany Jesus at the foot of the Cross knowing full well that he may also be killed and yet he was the only one not to receive martyrdom. Jesus gave the other apostles a second chance to prove themselves and gave John the honour of living a long life of servitude looking after our Lady and writing several books of the New Testament."* Maybe that was the kind of life he expected for himself.

During those two years of secondary school, Pedro continued to get excellent marks. Now he saw that his new vocation prompted him to help his friends more and bring them closer to God. One of them was a bit special. He was a smart boy, but he found it difficult to mix with people of his own age because he felt more comfortable with older people. Pedro's brothers found him a bit of a bore. Pedro insisted that they had to treat everyone with affection and found a way to talk to this friend about the things that interested him most.

He also had a friend who was a Catholic but had never practised his faith. Pedro devoted a lot of time to him until he began to accompany him to Mass, explaining the faith to him and transforming it into something more practical. As his friend liked photography, Pedro decided to accompany him one day to photograph the snow. He wasn't wearing proper clothes and was frozen stiff. Thus, he endured that Siberian spell and said nothing until his friend had taken more photographs than a National Geographic reporter.

Pedro knew how to bring out the best in each one. Nothing stopped him when it came to helping his friends. One of them, Lawrie Hughes, explained that when he fell ill and stopped going to school for a while, *"Pedro was the guy on the phone catching up with me and making sure I was all right, and this is something I won't forget"*. Lawrie's parents remembered Pedro *"who made everyone he met feel important"*. The day after his death, that same friend wrote on social media: *"My best friend passed away yesterday, but he'll always be that person pushing me, and many others, to do and be better. You are a special man, who won't be forgotten."*

After his death, his parents discovered how many people there were who considered Pedro their *"best friend."* People of all ages and conditions who came to know Pedro at different stages of his life. They all agreed on his capacity to love, to be aware of the needs of others and find ways to meet them.

Another of his talents was his ability to engage with any topic that interested others. Whether it was a 7-year-old boy, a beggar in the street, a university professor or the Bishop of Leeds. From the most intellectual topics to the most mundane, he always found something to spark the attention of whoever he was talking to and allow them to enjoy his company.

Pedro liked to learn about social issues around the world and took every opportunity to learn from people. Patrick commented that Pedro liked to ask him questions about Nigeria, his home country. However, when he answered them, he discovered that Pedro was already very knowledgeable as he had had many similar conversations with his Nigerian friends in school.

Pedro had a special magnetism and leadership which he used to help his friends become interested in the needs of others. He helped them to help. In the summer of 2013, he convinced a group of friends to make good use of their free time during the holidays by lending a hand to people in need. With five other friends he showed up one morning at the house of an old lady whose garden had become a jungle. They spent the day tidying the garden and fixing the outside of the house. By evening, although exhausted, dirty and smelling like sweaty socks, they all agreed that it had been a great plan and everyone wanted to do it again.

Part of his appeal derived from his devotion and his Christian life. A boy from the parish who was to receive the Sacrament of Confirmation was so impressed to see Pedro praying before the Blessed Sacrament that one day he approached him and asked him to be his sponsor. When Pedro accepted, the boy's smile said it all.

Pedro was very good at telling jokes and stories and had a special ability to see the funny side of any situation. Many of us remember his account of an accident in October 2013 that made all of us who listened to him cry with laughter. On a trip to London with three other Spaniards in a borrowed car, and while he was dozing in the back seat, they hit another vehicle that had stopped at a traffic light.

When the police arrived, the driver and co-driver could not make themselves understood in English. To add insult to injury, they didn't know whose car it was, they had no address in the UK, and they didn't even know their own phone numbers! The policeman thought they were kidding him and raised his voice at them to take him seriously. Pedro decided to come to the rescue since he was the only one who spoke English. But when he was asked for his phone number, he couldn't remember it either. He turned to one of them and asked him, in Spanish, to make a missed call in order to see his number. The policeman, his patience worn thin and by now at the end of his tether, began to shout once more that he was serious. Thank God, Pedro managed to clarify and defuse the situation so it did not escalate further.

Despite being Spanish, Pedro had a very English character. He spoke English with a Northern accent and did not hide his discomfort at the emotional effusiveness of some Spaniards when they met. However, he had often expressed his intention of moving to Spain for his university studies. Both his parents and the directors in Greygarth reminded him of the great apostolate he could do in the United Kingdom. Aware that God was asking him to stay in Britain, he put aside his preferences without any fuss. He made the decision to stay and never mentioned the subject again.

That was always his attitude. If he could help, he helped. No fuss. Without attracting attention. Without expecting thanks or acknowledgement of any kind.

With his top exam grades, Pedro could choose the university he wanted. He thought about applying for a place at Cambridge, but when he found out that there was still no Opus Dei centre in that city, he looked for other options. He went to visit Oxford to see if he should try to go there but he thought the atmosphere in that university city was a bit gloomy and so, he decided to apply for a place at Imperial College in London to study Chemical Engineering.

In January 2018, upon learning that Pedro had died, the professor who interviewed Pedro four years earlier, when applying for a place at Imperial College, wrote to his parents: "*I searched my interview notes and found the following comments after I interviewed him. 'The best of the five students I interviewed. Discussed his experience in EMED Tartessus in mines of Rio Tinto. Explained very well about processing copper ore and use of cyclone for separation. This is the student we are looking for.*"

In September 2014 he moved to Netherhall House, a university residence in London, to start his degree and in a short time he had made dozens of friends. Although he was only in London for three months, the mark he left at Netherhall and Imperial College was indelible.

During his short stay at Netherhall he did a great apostolate among the residents who lived there and with his fellow university students. One of them sent him a message shortly after he was diagnosed with cancer:

"*Hey Pedro, I heard about what you're going through and I just wanted to let you know that you're in my prayers. You may not have realised it, but meeting you has had a significant impact on my life. Seeing you hold your head up high about being a Christian inspired me to do the same. You inspired me to take that step towards becoming a faithful Christian – not just in Church but also in my daily life.*" Pedro hid that message out of humility, but his father found it at a later date.

In that autumn of 2014 everything was going great. In fact, a few months earlier, in a conversation with the director, Pedro commented that he felt *"too privileged"*, that everything was going well for him: his vocation, family, friends, his studies... And he said that, considering all this, it had occurred to him in prayer to ask Our Lord for a cross with which he could somehow pay for all that he had received.

Little could he, and those who were with him, imagine how God would answer that prayer.

4. The Cross

Since May 2014 Pedro had begun to notice a growing pain in his lower back. In August, when he went to Spain, the pain subsided quite a lot and he was even able to play football and practise sports. But upon returning to England in September, the pain returned with a vengeance. He tried different therapies, even going to an osteopath, but the pain did not decrease. One day, whilst playing football at the beginning of December, he realised that he could no longer run. He discreetly left the match and sat on the sidelines to wait for the others to finish the game.

A week before Christmas, Pedro took part in a retreat that I preached. Since I had studied medicine before my ordination, Pedro came to see me because he said that the pain would not let him sleep. I gave him a painkiller and suggested he go to the doctor when he got back home. A few days later he went on an excursion with other young numeraries. After walking several miles, the others noticed that he was limping and it hurt him to walk. When asked about it, Pedro downplayed it and said it was because he was studying a lot. At one point when they came to a stream that had to be jumped, they realised that Pedro could not cross it alone and they had to help him pass to the other side.

Pedro didn't say anything to anyone until after the diagnosis, but for over a month he hadn't been able to lie down in bed properly and he couldn't sleep. Nor could he sit for more than 15 minutes at a time and so he studied standing up. No one had any idea what he was going through because he never complained.

On Sunday December 28, he went to Mallorca with his parents and brothers to visit their relatives. The pain gave him no respite. Even so, he wanted to go fishing and had almost convinced everyone in the family when his grandmother told him over the phone to stop all that nonsense about going fishing and go immediately to the hospital accident and emergency department. A doctor friend of the family received him there. An X-ray revealed the unmistakable image of a bone tumour larger than 15cm in the pelvis. Upon seeing it, both his father and the doctor, who had often gone diving with Pedro, were unable to hold back their tears.

His parents decided not to tell him anything for the time being and they returned immediately to Manchester. Back in England, more tests were done and the diagnosis was confirmed. The osteosarcoma was in a very difficult position to operate. Finally, through tears, his parents explained everything to him. Upon receiving the news, seeing his mother cry, Pedro embraced her and said, *"Mum, you have always taught me that Jesus gives the Cross to his friends. I have already given my life to God with my vocation."*

After saying that, his mother commented, Pedro took some tablets, went to bed and slept very peacefully. He was beginning his climb to Mount Calvary which would last the next three years.

Those words to his parents would be the key to interpreting his entire life. Pedro saw an opportunity to embrace the Cross and continue to offer his pain and suffering for the Pope, for the Church and for souls.

The tumour pressed on his spinal cord and some nerves. The pain it must have been causing was evident on the X-ray and it was clear that the tumour had been growing for a long time. When asked why he had not said anything before when he felt those pains, Pedro answered simply: *"Yes I did say it… I said it to God. I was offering everything for the Pope, for the Church and for souls."*

Pedro gave up his degree course at Imperial College and returned to Manchester to receive treatment at the Christie Hospital, which has a team specialising in young cancer patients. He was immediately given painkillers and sleeping pills while awaiting the chemotherapy treatment he was to receive. For the first time in months, he slept without pain. On January 12, Pedro woke up without any symptoms that might remind him of his illness. Entering the kitchen and finding breakfast without sugar, without salt and without a long list of condiments, Pedro smiled and said: *"Wow! I had almost forgotten that I have cancer."*

The first cycle of chemotherapy hit him hard. He lost 20 kilos and experienced nausea and frequent vomiting. He had to follow a very unpleasant diet, but he never – literally *never* – complained. He kept his usual sense of humour. His loss of weight meant that for the first time his younger brothers weighed more than he did. When this was mentioned to him, Pedro pointed to his head and said, *"The important thing is what is up here... in that you do not surpass me."*

The doctors were alarmed at the sudden weight loss. Unable to stop the trend, they commented that they would weigh him again the following day and if he continued to lose weight, they would have to feed him through a tube. Pedro didn't like the idea. When the nurse came to weigh him the next day, it turned out that he had put on a little weight. The nurse, surprised, asked him how he had achieved it. Pedro, grinning from ear to ear, took two stones out of his pockets and said, *"With this!"* Finally, between laughs, they decided to dispense with the idea of the tube.

He lost weight. He lost his hair. He lost the academic year. But he didn't lose his smile. His cheerfulness comes out clearly in an Autograph book sent to him by his university classmates in London upon learning of his illness. Many messages referred to his joy and his smile, to his constant positive attitude, his promptness in helping others and to his palpable Christian faith. *"Everyone is missing you, your smile always lit up 9am,"* wrote one of them. *" I definitely miss your cheery spirit warming up the Chem Eng atmosphere,"* said another. *"You've had an enormous impact on all our lives and we're so thankful for that."* And another added: *"Pedro, Chem Eng is not the same without your little jokes and your warm smile!"*

But don't get it wrong: some think that a smile is purely a genetic feature. Either you have been given it or you haven't. But the smile is like a muscle; in fact, it is made by many muscles. And the muscles used for smiling are also strengthened by training. Among his notes from 2014, when he was already in pain but had not yet been diagnosed with the tumour, we read in numerous entries: *"Smile more"* or just *"Smile"* (this one particularly is repeated several times) or *"Be more cheerful"* or *"Sower of peace and joy."*

When his hair began to fall out, he decided to shave his head. That was, without a doubt, a great sacrifice. But without any fuss, he raised the trimmer with his right hand like someone holding a trophy, then, referring to the prelate of Opus

Dei, said, *"For the Father,"* and shaved himself.

He never complained, and if asked, he tried to draw attention away from the topic and change the subject. When visitors asked him if he was okay, he often replied, *"Don't worry. I'm not sick. It's only repairs"*...

One day the bishop was visiting Greygarth. Aperitifs were being served in the sitting room and as people entered the room they went to greet the bishop. Pedro at that time was on crutches and waited, quietly seated. When the bishop came to him and asked him what had caused his limp, Pedro, quite naturally and not wanting to become the centre of attention, told him that it was *"an injury"*.

On May 12 there was a Mass in honour of Blessed Alvaro del Portillo in Westminster Cathedral celebrated by Cardinal Vincent Nichols. Pedro and his family travelled to London to attend that Mass and visit friends. For some reason or other, they arrived at the cathedral an hour early. When back at his centre he explained that *"that was very strange."* With a mischievous grin, he said: *"we had to wait. Weird!"* And with a laugh, he added: *"My family never gets anywhere early"*.

As we have seen, Pedro was incapable of making anyone suffer and carefully drew a veil over the defects of others. One day he received a call from the osteopath who had treated him earlier, when it was thought that the pain was a muscle problem. The doctor asked him if he had got over that pain. Pedro explained very delicately that he had been diagnosed with osteosarcoma. There followed an uncomfortable silence but Pedro broke it by not giving importance to the matter and thanked him for his help and asked him not to worry because months before, no one would have suspected it was cancer.

Another trait of his personality was his good use of time. Since he would no longer be able to continue his university degree in London, he wondered what to do so as not to waste time. For those first few months after the diagnosis he was living at his parents' house and going to Greygarth daily. There he attended Mass in the afternoon and did repairs. It then occurred to him that he could continue with the studies of philosophy that he had been doing during the summers, and thus make progress in those subjects. A few days later, Fr Peter Haverty began giving him classes on the History of Medieval Philosophy.

5. The struggle

In his new situation Pedro kept looking for ways to respond to God urgently and generously. He wrote the following notes during a monthly recollection in those early months after diagnosis:

- *"God needs you now and you have to change now. You don't know when you will die."*

- *"If you died today, do you think you would enter Heaven?"*

- *"You have to study and do the norms and mortifications out of love of God."*

- *"Create a study timetable and avoid distractions."*

- *"We have to be **useful** instruments for God."*

- *"To go ahead in the apostolate at the university you have to study and give good example."*

- *"You have to do the examination of conscience well every day."*

- *"Use a notebook, not your phone, which you barely use."*

- *"Get to confession more often."*

- *"You lack a sense of urgency. You have no more time to lose."*

- *"You have to have prestige to be effective in the apostolate."*

- *"Time is glory."*

- *"We will have to account for wasted time."*

In August he attended a three-week course at Thornycroft Hall, near Manchester. He still had to go into hospital several times to continue his second set of chemotherapy sessions. Nevertheless, during the course he remained very cheerful. He played the comical host in birthday celebrations. A number of photos and videos of the activities from that course have already been widely circulated.

By the end of the first two cycles of chemotherapy it had become evident that his tumour was inoperable. The doctor explained to him, in front of his parents, that his tumour had no cure. For a while Pedro had worried about a proposed operation because it involved removing a large part of his pelvis and one leg, leaving the other leg immobile. Upon returning to the centre, he commented that the hopes of survival were *"very few, zero... practically none."* Pedro had had a hard time accepting the idea that after the operation he would spend the rest of his days without one leg, without a pelvis and the other leg paralysed. *"I want to die with two legs,"* he said one day, *"I want to go through those Pearly Gates walking, not in a wheelchair."*

One aspect of his struggle that never went unnoticed was his ability to endure suffering without complaining. A male nurse at the hospital explained how he had worked with many children and teenagers with cancer. He said, *"The little ones hardly ever complain; however, the teenagers never stop complaining... But Pedro is the exception. I have never heard the slightest complaint from him."*

Therapeutic answers were running out and hopes diminishing. However, the possibility of an experimental proton radiation therapy in Heidelberg, Germany unexpectedly arose. It would mean moving to Heidelberg for several weeks. But funding proved to be a stumbling block. The National Health Service could not finance the cost of the treatment that could exceed £100,000.

After numerous meetings, Pedro and his parents were told that the chances of a cure were very small and not worth the investment. Pedro was not immune to bad news and he later acknowledged that he had felt very low on the afternoon when he was told this. He would later comment that it was during this meeting that he realised the gravity of his situation.

Three days later, the Bishop of Shrewsbury went to visit him and left a prayer card with the words of our Lady to St. Juan Diego: *"Am I not here, I, who am your mother? Are you not under my shadow and shelter? Am I not the source of your joy? Are you not in the hollow of my mantle, in the crossing of my arms? What else do you need? Don't let anything worry you or grieve you."*

When he read them with his mother, he was so moved that they decided to recite those words every night. Abandonment marked the way in which Pedro and his family faced his illness. They put themselves in the hands of God and the Blessed Virgin and decided to take it all *"one step at a time"*. It gave him much peace knowing that everything would go as God would like. That inner peace was the fruit of abandonment.

They began to look for funding and part of the amount was raised, but the cost was still too high. Thanks be to God, after many meetings and thousands of prayers, almost at the last minute the funding was approved and the National Health Service covered most of the expenses.

Meanwhile the number of people praying for Pedro was growing. Prayers came from all over the world. The prelate of Opus Dei had mentioned this son of his several times in meetings with many people, asking them to pray for him. When asked if he thought the miracle could happen, Pedro replied with a broad grin and rapid-fire delivery, as if cracking a joke: *"Let us pray. But if I'm not cured, it's Heaven, so either way it's a winning situation"*.

The treatment in Heidelberg was neither invasive nor painful. Its aim was to burn away the bone with radiation. The discomfort came later, with the bone tissue dead and with a burn on the skin that took a long time to heal, of which he never complained. That treatment appeared to have left the tumour inactive. The effects lasted for a few months and Pedro was able more or less to resume his normal life.

For a period of time the wound on his skin caused by the radiation was the most significant discomfort he suffered. At one point, when the pain was especially intense, the director of Greygarth asked him to offer his discomfort for the Greygarth residents. Pedro smiled and said, *"Okay, I will offer for them in particular the pain in my bottom"*.

Shortly after that wound had healed, he began a second cycle of chemotherapy while trying to live a normal life. One day, at the end of August 2015, during a get together in Greygarth, Pedro said: *"You know, it was exactly a year ago that I came back from Barcelona, and then I went down to London to start my life at Netherhall and my university degree."* Then he added, *"It's been a great year".*

Everyone was speechless, then someone broke the silence saying: "You are such a positive guy!" Pedro felt obliged to clarify amid the laughter with a reference to popular culture: it was a bit like Lord Voldemort, he explained, *"Let's see... this year has been terrible, yes... but great!"*

In more difficult moments, when the pain was really intense, Pedro clung to the crucifix. *"Without the Cross,"* he said, *"none of this makes sense."* His father explained in a letter that one day it occurred to Pedro to ask himself: *"Why me? Why me?"* And with great simplicity he gave himself the answer: *"And why not me, who have faith and can offer it?"*

No matter how much pain he suffered, Pedro always tried to fulfil his duties. In October 2016, when the pelvic discomfort started to return strongly, Pedro had to finish a university assignment. Unable to bear the agony seated, he tried to type standing up. He experimented with many postures, but the pain did not cease. Finally, he ended up dictating the work to someone else, while lying on the ground, first face up and then face down, managing to send off his work just in time. When he got the mark back, Pedro was surprised at how good it was.

"One day he was in a lot of pain," says Chema, *"and he confessed to me that what he found most difficult*

was not being able to make any medium or long-term plans. I was amazed at how quickly he understood that he had to entrust himself to St. Joseph, "Patron Saint of temporary situations," as we agreed to call him."

He worked hard. At one stage he found himself with a bit of free time so he decided to go and help out at *The Cedars* school in London, whilst living at Kelston Study Centre, near Balham. There he set out to lend a hand in any way he could: rehearse a play, invigilate study, help students with difficulties and even help correct exams. He could sometimes be seen in the staff room, deep in concentration, correcting a pile of exam papers, without complaining about the exceptionally hot weather at the time.

"Pain is a mystery," he wrote in his notes one of those days, *"and yet the Christian with faith knows how to discover in the darkness of suffering, his own and others', the loving and provident hand of his Father God who knows more and sees further. Whoever has faith somehow understands the words of St. Paul: «To those who love God, all things are for the good»."*

Since his duty was to study, he tried to protect his study and work time. Sometimes, he studied as much as he could in the morning before taking his pain-killing medicines because he knew that after taking them, he would feel drowsy and would no longer be able to study really hard.

Because of his illness, many people began to visit him. He always felt quite uncomfortable being the centre of attention and he much disliked the "*Selfie Phenomenon*": suddenly it seemed everyone wanted to have a picture with him. But he accepted it as another sacrifice to offer up. He could see that those photos were important to people and he let himself be photographed without worrying about whether he came out with hair or without hair, with bags under his eyes, or looking pale, skinny or sleepy.

He also found demonstrative expressions of affection very irritating: excessive hugs, outbursts of laughter, noisy shouts and clapping, in a word "*Fuss*". He endured it all patiently with new people who came to visit him, but he did not hesitate to nip it in the bud with those he knew well. To them he would say, "*Please, no fuss.*"

During difficult moments, he relied a lot on prayer and the messages that people sent him. He was particularly pleased by the letters he received from the Father, the prelate of Opus Dei. On February 12, 2015, he received one that made him cry. He told the director that that day had been very hard. He was dizzy, tired and fed up with the tasteless food he had to eat. That letter could not have been more timely. With great affection, the Father told him that he was relying on him especially and Pedro was very moved by this.

As we said, holiness does not consist in being perfect but in not giving up trying to achieve it. More than once he lost patience with people. When, in the midst of his pains, people tried to cheer him up with jokes or songs and started making a racket in his room, sometimes he would send them out, or tell them seriously: "*Enough of the jokes*". Soon after, remorseful, he would ask their forgiveness. This happened on several occasions.

He also struggled to be more sympathetic to the shortcomings of others. He didn't understand why one of the students in his hall of residence didn't study, or why another didn't get up in the morning, or why another lad had started using drugs or didn't try to socialise instead of staying in his room playing video games.

He found it particularly frustrating that some people who could pray – and sometimes wanted to – did not do so, or said they would go to Mass and did not go. Sometimes he found it difficult to understand that others had such a hard time doing things that he did so naturally, because he did not consider himself special in anything. "*If I can do it,*" he thought, "*how can he not do it?*"

In his notes he described his struggle: "*I have to be more forgiving with the struggles and shortcomings of others. Merciful as my heavenly Father is with me.*" During the years of his illness he learned to understand better the difficulties of others and improved greatly in the virtue of patience.

While trying to be merciful to others, he was very demanding of himself. On some occasions he expressed to the director his perplexity about not receiving corrections and wondered if it would be because people felt sorry for him. He asked to be corrected in *"everything and always,"* and said that they shouldn't hold their tongue; he wanted to be corrected because he needed to be holy and had no time to lose. He was always very grateful for the corrections he received.

6. Apostolate

From the beginning of his illness, Pedro's room began to be the most popular one in the hospital. Pedro decorated his room with a crucifix, a picture of the Virgin Mary and his smile. Very soon the influx of people caught the nurses' attention. *"Pedro's Room"* quickly became known throughout the hospital.

One day, in September 2015, Bill accompanied Fr Robert to give Holy Communion to Pedro in the Christie. They took down the wrong department details and they got lost in the big main building. Unable to find it, they asked some nurses for directions who told them that the department they were looking for didn't exist. Finally, when asked by the receptionist, they said that their friend was called Pedro.

"Oh, Pedro! Why didn't you say so?" said the man with a big smile, *"Everyone here knows Pedro!"* And he took them to Pedro's room which was on the other side of the hospital.

Pedro's ward in the *Christie Hospital* was full of young cancer patients, like him. Before long he had met and talked to most of them. As there were always people in his room, he sometimes asked them to leave him so he could chat privately with someone, or he would suggest they could do some praying while he talked to a patient in another room.

Impressed by his smile and his serenity, even mothers and fathers of the other young patients came to talk to him and ask for advice. On one occasion, when entering the room, someone found Pedro asleep, while another young man with cancer was sitting next to him. Asked if he was talking to Pedro, the young man replied, *"No. He is asleep. I come to see him because being close to him brings me peace."*

Pedro's door was always open to everyone. To help lift spirits, every Wednesday there was a pizza night in the recreation room on Pedro's floor of *The Christie Hospital*. With the doctors' permission, patients could bring friends, have a pizza and watch a film together. It was a way of radiating some light in a difficult environment. As a result of his chemotherapy, Pedro lost his taste for pizza after a few weeks. But he always encouraged everyone to come and have a good time together, even if at some point he had to retire because he wasn't feeling well.

The number of visits was growing, especially from friends. Friends of all ages. Believers and non-believers. Priests and professed atheists.

Children and old people, many families, patients, doctors and nurses... As his brother Carlos said, his room *"reminded me of a scene from the Marx brothers in the film «A Night at the Opera», when loads of people were piling into a cabin in a ship. I'm surprised that the staff in the Christie didn't kick us out! I was always struck how in the midst of his own intense pain he was always interested in the problems of others and always willing to help."*

If there is one special virtue that everyone recognised in Pedro, it was friendship. *"Whoever has a friend has a treasure,"* Pedro wrote in the script of a talk he gave to Greygarth's students. He explained: *"A good friend knows you inside out and vice versa, but this can only be achieved by talking and spending time together. It's through our friendship that we talk about deep, important things such as religion."* He argued that, in the end, friendship, loving people, is already apostolate and that we help people with affection and example first. *"It's important to have good friends to help them but also because it helps us as well."* And he clarified: *"It's not that we have friends SO we can do apostolate. That wouldn't be true friendship."* He knew from experience that loving our friends is already doing apostolate.

The hospital staff were struck by the number of priests and bishops who came to see Pedro. He had a great love for the priesthood. He prayed a lot for priests, for their holiness and for their faithfulness. He was saddened to hear of priests who were very lonely and prayed especially for them. He commented on several occasions that if he recovered sufficiently, he would consider asking the prelate to go to Rome with the intention of becoming a priest if that was God's Will. He even mentioned asking for a dispensation to be ordained before finishing his studies, *"because I have no time to lose."*

One of the bishops mentioned that visiting Pedro was like going to see the Pope, because Pedro asked them about the number of seminarians, how to make them souls of prayer, to be faithful and holy, or if they had thought about how to promote more vocations and fill the seminary. Pedro always promised his prayers for those intentions.

In March 2015, three months after his diagnosis, he took a trip to London to see his friends from university and Netherhall House again. He wanted to make sure that, even if he was no longer in London, they could still be in contact with someone who would help them get closer to God. He spoke to others continuously, going out of his way to welcome all those who wanted to see him – and there were many. On his first night in London, he stayed up talking one-to-one with various people until he was reminded that it was well past his bedtime.

The next day, at 6:55, he was up and ready to do his prayer with everyone else. Throughout his illness he always made an effort to do his prayer and attend Mass in the centre, with the rest of the house. Often he was the first to arrive at the oratory before the morning prayer, even if he had hardly slept the night before, or had been vomiting. It would have taken much more than this to prevent him from joining the others at prayer the following morning. And if you asked him why he didn't just stay in bed, he would say, *"After being in the hospital I have realised that I will not always have the blessing of being able to pray with others before the Blessed Sacrament or to have Mass in my own home."*

There were people who considered him a saint and, to his embarrassment, some even said so to his face. Pedro always reacted quickly and said that it needed much more to be holy. One day he told his mother, *"I'm not going to die yet. Only the good die very young."*

When his mother reminded him of those words a few weeks later in front of several people, Pedro blushed and added, *"I still have a lot of time left."* And it was evident that he had no intention of wasting a second.

The nurses were a good case in point. Pedro learned their names, asked them about their families and promised to pray about their worries and concerns. As he spent periods of time alternately in hospital and at home, and nurses often changed wards, he would not see them for months on end or even for over a year. But he still remembered their names and the people he had been asked to pray for. There were nurses who came from other wards to see him because word had spread that they had to meet this young man with a permanent smile.

Pedro gave them no respite. When they asked him to pray for someone, he in turn asked them for prayers. He would ask them about their faith, about their religious practice. He encouraged Catholics who did not practise to return to Mass, to confession. And when they came back to see him, he again reminded them.

On one occasion a Catholic nurse opened her heart to him. She was going through a difficult family situation and was very unhappy. Pedro asked her, *"Are you going to Mass?"* When she replied that she was no longer going, Pedro told her, *"Maybe that's why you are not happy."* That woman promised to begin practising her faith again and kept her promise.

When asked to pray for someone, he typed their name on his phone. He had a list longer than a giraffe's scarf, and he read it from time to time in his prayer to renew his intentions and remember the names.

As his illness lasted three years and he was frequently hospitalised, he came to know many people very well and several returned to religious practice thanks to Pedro. Some were surprised that Pedro remembered their name and family circumstances, even though it had been more than a year since they had last seen each other.

A little detail that never passed unnoticed by those who were with him him was his refinement in dealing with younger female doctors and nurses. With them, he was careful to keep his distance and avoided looking at them whenever possible. In a very natural way, when they weren't talking to him, he would look away.

He had temptations against the virtue of holy purity, like everyone else. And he was relentless in his fight. Among his personal notes, he mentions many battles, such as this one: *"Temptations of purity during the night and, sometimes, also during the day. I acted well. I was tired and that's why it costs more. Guarding my sight needs to improve. My heart, better: I try to put my heart into God more often."* And on 23 March 2016, he wrote: *"At night, get out of bed when it gets too much."*

A couple of months later he wrote: *"Beware of concupiscence. Don't spend too much time on the computer"*. Another day: *"Control the imagination. Focus on today and now. Take the fight away from the main walls of the fortress. Temperance."* And again a few weeks later: *"Control the imagination. Focus on today and now. Take the struggle away from the main walls of the fortress. Temperance."*

Pedro on the day of his First
Holy Communion with
Johnny McCusker.

With his cousin Pelayo Arenas Bastero

Breeding birds.

Performing during a talent show.

With his brothers and his cousins Venzal Ballester.

With his brothers and some cousins Ballester Nebot.

With his grandad Pedro Ballester.

During a summer camp with the club in Wales.

During the World Youth Day in Madrid.

With his brother Carlos during UNIV in Rome.

With Pablo and Andy.

«The accounts won't
wait for my pains to
disappear»

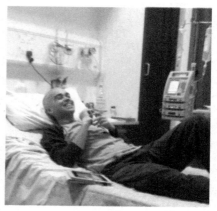

His constant smile
was captivating.

On the ferry in Scotland with some friends.

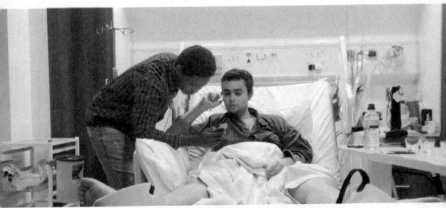

With Gitahi, one of the residents of Greygarth.

The whole family in Rome.

The family with Don Javier Echevarría.

In The Cedars School.

During a get-together in Netherhall.

With all the residents in Netherhall.

August 2017, the last time he was with the prelate of Opus Dei, Don Fernando Ocáriz.

With Mum and Carlos.

Selfie with Don Mariano Fazio.

During the last days he was mostly unconscious.

During his funeral celebrated by archbishop Arthur Roche.

His brother Carlos collected his posthumous title of Masters in Chemical Engineering.

Turn Then Most Gracious Advocate, Thine Eyes Of Mercy Towards Us

Love Means Deeds

PEDRO BALLESTER ARENAS
22 May 1996 - 13 January 2018

Pedro's remains rest in a cemetery in Manchester.

Pedro Ballester with his parents.

In November 2015 with Pope Francis.

7. Fidelity

In June 2016, when Pedro had been battling with cancer for a year and a half, the director of Greygarth residence moved to Oxford. In Greygarth there was a fairly young leadership team – called the local council – consisting of a director, an assistant director and a secretary together with the priest of the residence. That move brought about some changes and Greygarth needed a new secretary. The directors asked Pedro if he would be willing to fill the position. And he accepted without any fuss:

"Once you say yes to God... it's just a matter of continuing to say yes," he explained.

It is rare for a member of the local council to be appointed without having received two years of initial formation, but in Pedro's case, it was born of necessity. When he told me about it, he said, *"Pray a lot for Greygarth, Father. Things have to be very bad for me to have to be the secretary."*

But things were not going badly at all, and even less so with him in the local council. There he put himself at the service of all by learning fast and fulfilling his duty. Sometimes, when he returned from the hospital after a course of treatment, he would be very weak and so the local council met in his room while he, from his bed, took minutes of the meeting.

To meet this new challenge, he knew he had to work harder at his prayer. In his personal notes, he jotted down: "*My new duties are beyond me. Things are going to get harder. I have to pray more.*"

Likewise, having to take care of Greygarth's accounts, he needed to learn something about bookkeeping. Fr Andrew, who had experience with accounting, lent him a hand. It was not uncommon to see him at the accounts on his return from a long hospital stay or when he was feeling quite unwell. "*The accounts won't wait for my pains to disappear,*" he once commented.

While studying, he did whatever people asked of him or volunteered to do what others could not. He received families who came to visit Greygarth looking for university students' residences and put the house rules in writing so that those interested in applying to the residence could read them. He bought chairs, analysed the year's electricity bills to see if it was worth changing supplier, made purchases for the house, changed light bulbs, activated the electronic keys of the new residents... One day, the diary reads, "*Pedrito walked around the house with a mop, looking for the sources of the water leaks; there seems to be a leak near the toilet area on the first floor; not a leak in the plumbing, but in the waterproofing, so that the rain gets in."*

He also had a hand for fine work. One day he filed the spare key to the tabernacle because it wouldn't open the lock properly. With a tiny file, he discovered which tooth was not exactly the same and filed it slightly until the key worked perfectly.

Despite his condition, when his strength allowed, he could be found working in the Greygarth garden or doing repairs around the house or, sometimes, taking mail to a neighbour when it had been posted mistakenly in the Greygarth mailbox. While he was still able, he tried to serve naturally and without fuss.

In August 2016 he spent a month in Glasgow. Father Gonzalo González, an 85-year-old Opus Dei priest, was dying. Pedro was able to visit him several times. He himself wrote a letter to the Father in which he explained their first meeting:

"The first time I went to see him we entered the room and Fr Gonzalo was awake, but he was looking at the ceiling and it seemed that he did not realise we had come in. Jack and I were talking and then he introduced me to Fr Gonzalo, and when he said my name, he looked at me and with a lot of effort he asked me, "How are you?" This moved me a lot. I replied that I was very

well. We had never seen each other but I realised that he had prayed a lot for me and that he kept on praying."

The virtue of fidelity, like one's mother tongue, is learned by being thrown into it. And Pedro commented on how impressed he was by that meeting with a faithful priest who was dying of old age, worn out, squeezed dry like a lemon.

But faithfulness is never fully achieved on this earth. It is a lifelong battle that lasts until the final moment. Pedro was well aware of his mistakes and miseries; after the examination of conscience, he would often refer to his inner struggle. The depth of this struggle is revealed in the personal notes he wrote on his phone during his prayer, during his examination of conscience and at other times of the day.

In those notes, he wrote to Jesus or sometimes to himself in the second person, as if talking to himself. In January 2016 he wrote: "*You must have ambition and work as if everything depends on you. And then pray as if it was only up to God. And that's it. Today something happened that you could not prevent and you feel guilty and you are very embarrassed. Water under the bridge. Now Forward! To work, to study and to do apostolate.*"

How beautiful is the Christian's struggle when one does not give up!

Many notes show how demanding he was on himself. Soon after starting, he wrote on his phone: *"You're doing well, but you can do much better. Timetable. Don't waste time. Pray more, love the Lord. You are still ashamed to talk about God and Jesus in front of people. Get to know your Faith better, talk to the residents of Greygarth, don't be afraid... Go to confession and start again."*

On his examination, a few days later: *"Tuesday no Rosary, I was too tired. Didn't contact friend to cancel appointment. Rushing my mother when we talk on the phone, she talks a lot and I get tired. Imagination, when alone, in bed."* And again a few weeks later: *"I forgot the Preces for several days except yesterday and today. I also forgot the contemplation of the mysteries except yesterday when I remembered, after that, I forgot again."*

On the outside, it was all normal activity. Inside it was a struggle. Greygarth's diary of February 8 2016, refers to Pedro taking care of the house, going over the centre's accounts, playing chess with Greg and Nico, working in the garden. However, Pedro wrote on his phone that day: *"Today I don't feel like doing anything."* Well, he did manage to do lots of things, whether he felt like it or not!

Sometimes it was difficult for him to go to bed and he would stay up checking his phone for messages. As we find in a personal note from his examination of conscience: *"Look after the night period well, straight to bed once in the bedroom."*

He wrote down his Lenten resolutions for that year on his phone:

- Look after the norms of the plan of life

- Control the imagination

- Work/Study: Study plan

- Apostolate.

Pedro created an affectionate atmosphere around him. He treated all the Greygarth residents with affection, but even more so the other members of Opus Dei. He really went to town with them.

On numerous occasions, Pedro commented that he was offering his life for vocations: asking God to send many new ones and keep those that had already come faithful. He frequently repeated the aspiration: *"Serviam!"* (I will serve). That was St. Michael the Archangel's prayer to counter the rebellion of Satan who did not want to serve God, uttering his characteristic *"Non serviam!"* (I will not serve). Pedro's intention was to serve God as He wanted to be served. Some days he found it harder to say it. The day before one of his hospital admissions he said to his mother: *"Mum, help me to say «Serviam!»"*, and so they both said it together.

8. Sense of Humour

During Pedro's illness the atmosphere in Greygarth was very relaxed. One day Iñaki, one of the residents, had put on his well-known – and much commented upon – green trousers and the whole building was pervaded with a powerful scent of perfume. Apparently, *someone*, to play a joke on him, had left an air freshener on top of Iñaki's trousers in his wardrobe for him to find there. But the residents all went off on their Easter holidays and forgot about the matter. When everyone returned and Iñaki started wearing the unfortunate trousers again, they emanated a strong perfumed scent wherever they went. Jokes in the house continued for weeks because everyone knew whether Iñaki had gone to the oratory, to the dining room, had sat on a chair or passed through a corridor because of the tremendous scent trail that his trousers left behind.

Several residents were charged with the crime. The animosity towards those green trousers was heard from a distance. The defendants had to plead their innocence in a public trial during the get-together. The mystery took several weeks to solve. One day, almost a month later, Pedro told Iñaki that his trousers were *still* smelling. Iñaki realised at that very moment that Pedro had never defended his innocence. Pedro, knowing that he had been found out, began to laugh out loud – and all of Greygarth with him.

Pedro had given Fr Robert a bottle of whisky years earlier. Being Scottish, Fr Robert liked it very much and taught Pedro to distinguish both the good from the bad and the different types. Soon Pedro also began to enjoy having a little drink from time to time. One day some friends came to see him at the hospital and brought him a bottle. They got several plastic cups and proposed a toast. Evidently, a hospital is not the best place to drink whisky, and upon hearing the footsteps of an approaching nurse, Pedro gave orders to hide the proof of the crime.

When the nurse appeared in the doorway, she was a little surprised to see the commotion. Everyone was standing erect in formation, as if in the army, with their hands suspiciously hidden behind their backs. Pedro had just enough time to pass his cup to someone else while smiling at the nurse. When she left, Pedro said to them, "*You will get me kicked out of the hospital!*"

In February a retreat brochure was printed for Greygarth showing an old photo of Pedro and his brother Javier, their mouths covered with adhesive tape. The photo had been taken a year earlier, as a joke, but it appeared in the brochure to remind us that it was a silent retreat. Pedro laughed when he saw the photo and commented: *"If you want silence on the retreat, you'd better not take my brothers."*

His hospital room was often full and the gatherings there always included laughter that could be heard from the nearby corridors. On one occasion, after he finished the second cycle of chemotherapy, a couple of doctors came to see him in the room. Among other data, he was told that in a week he had lost 5 kg. Pedro smiled and said: *"Well, then, this diet must be patented because it works wonders!"* One of the doctors could not stop laughing while the other, couldn't hide his amazement at Pedro's resilience and how, despite the suffering, Pedro kept his sense of humour intact.

One day four friends came by train from London to see him. They were late and called him on the phone to find out if they could attend Mass with him. Pedro checked the parish Mass times and saw that they would arrive just before the midday Mass. Jack asked, *"Will you be able to go with them?"* Pedro began to feel his body with his hands, as if searching for something, and with a smile replied: *"Let's see... umm... I think so... I'm still alive!"*

Hospital kitchens are not usually given Michelin

stars. Although he never complained, after so many days with the same food, he felt ready to eat the hospital towels. His parents and other visitors tried to bring him some "food supplements." Specifically, one thing he really liked was sushi. Sometimes those who visited him brought him sushi or sandwiches from the shop downstairs, where there was a special offer after 4pm to sell the food that could no longer be sold the next day.

By telephone from his room, Pedro directed the operation with military precision. He would send someone to the store to find out what was on offer. When the price of sushi dropped below £1.80 or he liked the sandwiches on offer, he approved the purchase: *"Green light! I repeat: Green light! Transaction approved. Operation Sushi **is a go**."*

If the sushi was not on offer or the sandwich prices did not convince him, he communicated his instructions unequivocally: *"Abort! I repeat! To all units: abort the mission!"*

One day there was a birthday celebration in Greygarth. People did comic sketches, sang or told jokes. At one point it was his brother Carlos' turn and he started to get carried away. While everyone was bursting with laughter, Pedro said to him, *"Carlos. We've already talked about you not doing that anymore."*

Carlos, a little confused, asked him: *"Not doing what?"*

"Embarrassing me," Pedro replied.

And later, recalling the incident, he explained: *"Carlos' problem is that he has no shame... I have all of his and mine put together."*

His joy showed even when no one was watching. Pedro could sometimes be heard singing or humming a song in the hospital shower or as he walked up and down a Greygarth corridor.

In February 2017 there was a talk given to Greygarth residents about how to get a project done. Among the students was one who had been asking for prayers for a long time to find a girlfriend. Pedro did not miss the opportunity and asked him seriously: *"Some people have been trying for many years to find a wife. At what age, do you think, should they give up?"*

When he had to sit down because of the pain, he always said he was sorry for not being able to help. One day the priest told him that he *was* helping. He helped with his prayers and his pains. *"You are the heart that beats for others,"* the priest told him. To which Pedrito replied: *"Well, this heart is quite* arrhythmic."

Many times when his friends went to visit Pedro, they ended up playing cards or chess with him. In that relaxed atmosphere, Pedro held very amusing conversations and had a great time.

Thus, with great naturalness, he took advantage of these visits, allowed people to have fun and at the same time helped them to consider great ideals. Those of us who visited him did not have the impression of going to see a sick person, but of visiting a friend, who at that time happened to be sick. As he wrote in one of his personal notes: *"Don't forget that illness and studies are circumstances. What really matters is vocation, fidelity, becoming a saint."*

A mystery that accompanies Spaniards living abroad – and that intrigues many – is the irresistible magnetism of the Spanish potato omelette (as for the onion, I leave that up for debate) or some slices of quality Serrano ham. Pedro was always grateful when such delicacies were brought to him in hospital, sidestepping all health controls. But whatever delicacies came, he always offered them to others and barely tasted a morsel himself. Despite having many pains to offer, he also wanted to offer sacrifices that were not imposed on him, but that he could choose to take on freely. As we have seen, Pedro did not use his illness as an excuse to reduce his list of mortifications.

Joy, like any virtue, is demonstrated when it's hard to be joyful, just as strength is shown when you hit a rough patch, or sincerity shown when telling the truth gets you into trouble. Not surprisingly, suffering, pain and death test one's joy. Therefore, as he approached the end, when the pain had become really intense and it was difficult for him to smile, Pedro commented: *"My battle now is to die joyfully."*

On more than one occasion, when someone saw him a little sad, he was asked the reason why. His response was: "*It hurts me not to be able to live a normal life. It hurts me to be bothered by the laughter of others. I wasn't like that before.*"

By the beginning of 2017, all possible healing measures had been exhausted. The cancer was active again and spreading once more. The doctors told him that he had only months to live. It was like a slap in the face. Until that day, Pedro used to explain, he still had hopes that the tumour could be controlled. From then on, everything changed. He described to those who were with him that he was now waging "*a mental battle against cancer*" in which he must not break down, because many depended on him. It was a very hard struggle to remain joyful and to continue until the end without giving in, without losing his optimism. But now that optimism took on a different focus: it was the struggle to die a saint.

"*It's no longer just about going to heaven, but about taking many to heaven. That demands much more.*"

A few days after being told he had months to live, he came across a group of five priests who had come to attend a talk. It was February 2017. Pedro knew them and stayed for a while chatting. Soon the subject of his funeral came up (it is not clear how) and Pedro began to joke about what he expected from priests who would concelebrate his funeral Mass. Fr John suggested that they sing the *Kumbaya*. Pedro was amused and asked the priests to sing it there and then *"to see how it sounded"*; if it didn't work, they would have to play an mp3 recording instead. They all ended up rolling with laughter.

When they managed to compose themselves again, one of the priests asked him how he had taken the news. Pedro replied that he had received it much better than his family. He explained that when the doctor told him the day before that the cancer had returned and he had less than a year to live, he made an effort to smile because his mother was with him. *"It's always harder for the family,"* he said.

What surprised those priests most was that Pedro recounted it with a big smile and great serenity, making sure that they enjoyed that meeting and that his presence did not spoil the party. Quite the opposite: those priests have not yet forgotten how emotional that encounter was.

Among the frequent intentions for which Pedro prayed and offered sacrifices were priestly vocations, vocations of women as assistant numeraries and, in general, the faithfulness of all souls to their vocation.

9. Self-giving

"To give oneself sincerely to others is so effective that God rewards it with a humility filled with cheerfulness," St. Josemaría wrote. Pedro was irrefutable proof of that truth.

Pedro had the knack of always directing attention to others. He was the one who asked how things were going for the visitor, and when he was asked to pray for some intention, he always remembered what they told him. On one occasion a nurse had to come and help him because he had vomited. Despite feeling very sick, Pedro recognised her immediately and asked her about her son's exams which had worried her so much in their previous conversation.

On another occasion, Luke, a Protestant friend of Pedro's, brought along one of his own friends (also a Protestant) to meet Pedro at Greygarth. In the get-together after the meal, Pedro spoke naturally of some of the conversations he had had with nurses and doctors in the hospital. He spoke to everyone about God, Jesus, the meaning of life, the power of prayer... One story followed another and Pedro was talking for almost an hour. At the end, fascinated by what he'd heard, Luke's friend commented, "*I have met a Christian on fire!*"

Going to visit him was always a pleasure. Felix brought his friend James to meet Pedro. On leaving, James remarked, "*I feel much better now than when I came into the room*". Those who visited him came back delighted. One visitor came back saying that he was "*a real gift*", explaining that Pedro was always smiling, and you could see in his eyes that he was very happy. Another priest, Mgr John Walsh, who went to see him often, admitted that at first, he came with the intention of helping Pedro; but later, he said "*It does me good, to be honest; that's why I like to visit him so much.*"

It is important to realise that what may sometimes seem innate is nothing more than sheer practice. Rafael Nadal (to quote another famous name from Mallorca) doesn't play tennis well just because he won the genetic lottery, as if he didn't have to practise daily for hours and hours. At the end of the day, talent is a matter of practice and so is holiness. There are those who thought that it came naturally to Pedro to speak about God; that being *apostolic* is a gift that some have and others do not.

That is why it could come as a bit of a surprise to find so many of his personal notes in which he asked during his prayer to overcome human respect: *"Do not be ashamed to talk about God,"* he wrote during a retreat. This shows that in this too his weakness had to be overcome. After restarting his studies in Manchester, he wrote in his notes: *"You have to meet a lot of good people at university and invite them to retreats and meditations. To love them very much. Work hard."* And so he did.

That was what people perceived on the outside. But Pedro kept asking Our Lord in his prayer to lose his shame of speaking about God to others. At the end of a formation course he wrote in his prayer: *"Lord, I want to finish this course closer to you, with an eagerness for apostolate and for you to take away my human respect. Give me the grace to do what I have to do at all times."*

Holiness therefore consists in never giving up the fight. At times Pedro had to struggle to stop focusing on his own things and devote more time to other people, his family or the other residents of Greygarth. Among his notes are many like these: *"You have to fight in STUDY, MORTIFICATION, APOSTOLATE."* *"Look after the night time better, silence so as to pray at night. Go straight to bed."* *"Pride: don't get angry with people."* *"Help people to be holy: I need to correct them."* And with incisive persistence: *"Timetable. Timetable. Timetable"*.

In his time of meditation with God, he also prayed for his friends to see how he could help them more. And the best way to help others is always to start with oneself. He wrote one day in his prayer: *"You must set an example. You cannot demand from others what you do not demand of yourself.*" He applied this to his friends and to the other members of the Work: "*Think of my brothers in my prayer. One by one,*" he wrote. He also expected himself to be more demanding: "*Correct others when I see things that can improve. Don't look the other way!*"

Another aspect in which he had to struggle was being more natural. He soon realised that people treated him with deference; because he was sick, people treated him more kindly and he felt more watched. This sometimes led him to feel a bit self-conscious amongst people with whom he was less familiar. That is why he wrote one day in his examination: "*Act naturally at home. Be yourself.*"

At the same time he realised that, sometimes, there were those who treated him as if he were a celebrity and did not dare to approach him or start a conversation. At the start of one of the gatherings in which new people appeared, he wrote in his diary: "*Talk to the new ones.*"

One of the first people he met at Manchester University upon re-starting his degree in October 2015 was Ugo. He was French and it was his first week away from home. Pedro realised that he was very quiet and began to talk to him. Ugo explained that he missed his family very much. They spoke for a while as they walked around the campus. Ugo told him that he believed life had no meaning and ended in nothingness. Pedro asked him if he believed in God and Ugo said no. *"That's why you're sad,"* Pedro told him.

Later Pedro thought that perhaps he had been too blunt and began to pray for him. But the next day, very early, Ugo called him to ask if they could meet up again because he wanted to continue talking to him *"about the meaning of life and all that."*

The loss of his faculties made him suffer in many ways. One day his mother took him to college by car. When he got out of the car he saw a group of friends and hurried to reach them on his crutches. The pain was intense and that group of boys did not slow down, but Pedro did not stop. With great effort he managed to reach them and they entered the university together. When he finished and it was time to return home, he got into his mother's car where she was waiting for him, and he burst into tears. He could no longer even walk fast to catch up with the others.

It was almost instinctive for Pedro to offer his help. On one occasion he went to run an errand near Manchester city centre with his adapted car. When he was about to return, an old woman asked him for help to carry her shopping. Although Pedro was limping, the lady didn't seem to notice anything. Seeing that the distance was going to be considerable and that he wouldn't be able to carry the bags, Pedro offered to take the lady by car - and so he did.

When he dropped the lady off at her house and was on his way back home, a drunken cyclist, bottle in hand, fell over just in front of him. Pedro got out of the car to help him. He got back to Greygarth in the end, a bit late to dinner but ready to tell the story of his adventures.

His apostolate knew no bounds and he took advantage of every opportunity. On December 21, 2016, several Manchester United players went to visit the hospital where Pedro was. Among the players were Juan Mata, Ander Herrera and David de Gea. As they were Spaniards, Pedro took the initiative to show them round the floor. With his mother's help, he did not miss the opportunity to talk about Opus Dei, Greygarth and the importance of the formational activities held there.

Pedro was ready to do anything to help people. On one occasion, a nurse came to his room to give him a dose of morphine for the intense pain he was in. As Pedro was with a group of friends at that moment, he asked her to come back later. She did come back later, but another group had come and the same thing happened again. Finally, Pedro was on his own with just one other friend. The nurse came in again. To calculate the dose, she asked him, *"From zero to ten, how much does it hurt?"*

Pedro answered, *"Eight!"* The nurse put her hands to her head and went out to get the medicine. The person with him asked: "*But why didn't you ask for the medicine before?*" With great naturalness, Pedro replied: "*Because that medicine makes me sleepy and stops me from paying proper attention to people.*"

Pedro was loved by people because he loved people. One day, whilst travelling in the car, able to sit up only with great difficulty due to the pain, he nevertheless wanted to take a detour to pass through the town of a cancer patient he had met in hospital. That way, the next time they met, he would be able to talk to him about his hometown.

He was eager to get to know people. Shortly before his death he met Stephen. After talking for a while, Stephen commented that he would have liked to get to know him much better. Pedro suddenly felt sad, as if realising that he was running out of time to make friends, and he commented, "*Me too.*" A year later, no doubt as a result of Pedro's prayers, Stephen would enter the seminary to become a priest.

St. John Henry Newman said that a characteristic of a gentleman is to have "*his eyes on all his company*" and adds: "*his great concern being to make everyone at their ease and at home.*" Pedro fitted that definition perfectly.

A day before one of his stays in hospital, he invited some friends home to have a pizza with his parents. As one of them, Javier, was from Guatemala, Pedro recommended a very spicy pizza, thinking he would like it. But soon Pedro realised that Javier was spitting fire out of his mouth: the pizza was too spicy for him. Discreetly, Pedro suggested to the others that they let Javier have some of theirs so that he would not have to eat the whole of his pizza or be left hungry.

Sometimes, after long sleepless nights, due to his very aggressive treatments, pain, nausea and tiredness, Pedro would remain in bed, with his eyes closed, talking very little. However, when a doctor or nurse entered, he would draw strength from weakness and start talking to them quite naturally. The change never ceased to amaze those who were with him him.

Pedro was already very ill when one of his friends from the *Christie Hospital* died. Nevertheless, Pedro asked to be taken to his funeral. It took several hours by car, but he was keen to go because he knew his friend's family didn't practise any religion, and he wanted at least one person to be there to pray for him.

It was evident that Pedro loved people and enjoyed being with them. On one occasion when he was already very ill, the gathering in his room had lasted a long time. Someone made a gesture to get up and send everyone to bed, but Pedro said, *"Let's keep this going a little longer. I'm enjoying it a lot."*

In February 2017, Pedro already knew that he had less than a year to live. One day he told a fellow resident: *"It is useless to spend time calculating how much I have left. If I take it badly, I can lie in bed and wait for death to come and pick me up. But there are souls to save and God knows how much time He is giving me.*

10. Climbing Mount Calvary

Over and above his physical sufferings, Pedro offered many more moral sufferings for which, as he said, *"there is no morphine."* First, he suffered for his parents and brothers. It was very common for Pedro to say to those closest to him, *"Don't worry about me. Just pray for my parents."* He made the same request to many of us in similar words. Regarding the news of cancer coming back, he wrote to Archbishop Roche: *"it has hit my parents and my brothers very hard, I'm all right, as usual. It did come as a shock though and I'm worried about the pain and my ability to walk. It's very annoying to say the least. But I'm more worried about my family to be honest."*

He realised that his illness had absorbed the time and attention of his entire family. Pedro saw his parents and brothers cry on numerous occasions. He was aware that no one suffers totally alone. Like Jesus on Golgotha, lover and beloved suffer together. Those who love accompany the beloved to the summit and contemplate in agony the Calvary of the one they love.

His family suffered seeing him suffer. Pedro suffered seeing them suffer. But if God did not spare his Mother that bitterness, he does not spare his children either. Pedro's parents and brothers watched every moment of that battle from the front row. The vocation of his family was that of the Blessed Virgin, that of John and Mary Magdalen. It was even like that of the good thief Dismas at times, because seeing the one you love on the cross crucifies you too.

His parents would have wanted to carry that cross themselves. But Pedro's cross could not be carried by anyone else. They had theirs. After all, not even the Blessed Virgin could, no matter how much she wanted to, take away even a splinter of her Son's Cross. She was not there to carry the Cross of Jesus, but to carry her own (a mother's cross) at her Son's side. To be compassionate: *Compassion* comes from the Latin, *com-pati* "suffer with". Suffering is individual, but we can suffer with another, and that is always a comfort.

Allow me a reflection that I mentioned to Pedro on one occasion and can help those who suffer: *"Stabat Mater dolorosa,* **iuxta** *Crucem,"* says Scripture. The Mother *stood by* the Cross. But not **on** the Cross. She had hers. The nails that pierced the hands of Jesus also pierced the heart of his Mother. The insults that wounded Jesus, wounded his Mother. The thorns, the cold, the shame... everything affected the two in different ways. The spear pierced the Immaculate Heart of the Mother more than the Sacred Heart of the Son, since the Heart of Jesus was no longer beating and suffering, but Mary's was.

Pedro's room was like a Calvary. His parents, like 'The Mother' at the foot of the Cross, were there with their own cross; and his brothers (including those of Opus Dei) were like St. John and St. Mary Magdalen.

The Mystery of Suffering is like this. Each soul goes up Mount Calvary carrying their own cross. But it is a blessing to go accompanied by others who bear theirs. One of the greatest consolations of suffering is that Christ is not 'indifferent' to it. In fact, he is very 'different': Jesus weeps. That is the shortest verse in the Gospel: "Jesus wept" (Jn 11:35).

The Gospel passage on the death of Lazarus is in itself a whole mystery. Jesus is told that his friend is dying and He doesn't even move. When his friend dies, then Jesus sets out. He himself tells his disciples that Lazarus has died. Arriving in Bethany, Martha goes out to meet Him: "Martha said to Jesus, 'Lord, if you had been here, my brother would not have died'." She had a point.

But Jesus knows what He's going to do. Immediately the other sister, Mary, comes and reproaches Him with the same question: Why have you done this? "Lord, if you had been here, my brother would not have died." And then it happens:

"Jesus, seeing her weeping, and the Jews who accompanied her, also weeping, shuddered in spirit and was moved, and said, 'Where did you put him?' They said to him, 'Lord, come and see.' **Jesus wept.**"

Jesus didn't weep for Lazarus (He knew he was going to rise again). Jesus did not weep when He was condemned to death. We don't read in the Gospels that Jesus wept during the Passion. He doesn't seem to weep for Himself. But Jesus wept when He saw Mary weep.

The Heart of the Creator shudders at the tears of His children. A friend told me, *"I could only believe in a God who weeps. If He wasn't able to weep He wouldn't really be* **God**." He has a point.

We never shed our tears alone. God weeps with His children. It is as comforting to know that God can shed tears *with* us, as to know that God can shed Blood *for* us.

God does not take away our tears – but adds His own.

Did Jesus weep when he saw his Mother at the foot of the Cross? I know He did. His Mother's tears were a suffering added to the lashes and the spittle, the insults and slaps, to the nails and the thorns. Noble suffering is, more often than not, in the flesh of others. Who suffered most, Pedro or his parents? Everyone suffered terribly. Each one their own pain. Same Calvary; different cross.

Speaking of this, Pedro told me one day: *"Dying is much more difficult than I thought. What makes me suffer most is not the cancer, but the people."*

With his brothers, Carlos and Javi, he acted as the older brother that he was. Having to attend to so many people who came to see him, he tried not to forget his own. Among his personal notes we can read things like this: *"You have to spend more time with Javi and talk to him about school and the things he likes. Must call Carlos to talk to him as well. Look after Dad"*. He asked his brothers about their studies, their exams, their classes and their interests. He asked them to help more and not to create problems, to take care of their parents, to help them rest, to offer to take turns in accompanying him so that they could disconnect from time to time.

But the heart of a father and a mother never disconnects. Interestingly, when Jesus said that people in Heaven *"neither marry nor are given in marriage"* (*Mt* 22:30) and therefore there are no husbands and wives there, He did not modify the fact that for all eternity there will continue to be mothers and fathers, sons and daughters, brothers and sisters. That will never change.

11. Faithfulness on Calvary

Opus Dei numeraries can be incorporated from the age of 18 for a period of one year. Every year, on March 19, the feast of St. Joseph, if they so wish, they renew their dedication for another year. That is repeated for at least 5 years, after which they can ask for definitive incorporation by doing the "fidelity". On the day of their fidelity, they receive a ring.

The time for Pedro to do the fidelity would have been at the age of 23. Aware that he would die before reaching this date, Pedro asked if he could do his fidelity before. From Rome the prelate granted him a dispensation and it was planned to happen on 11 March 2017. But on that date he was feeling unwell and had to postpone it until the following day, March 12. The ceremony usually takes place in an oratory or church. That day the priest brought him Holy Communion in hospital and Pedro was able to make his promises before Jesus Sacramentally present. It was one more proof of love for his vocation.

The physical pains were becoming increasingly evident but he did not forget to offer them up and ask for prayer intentions. As he wrote one day to Chuma, a friend of his: *"Today the pain has been particularly bad. But I've been offering it up for various intentions. Do you have any intentions that I could pray for?"*

Dated 9 March 2017, Greygarth's diary explains: *"He finds it hard to get round to doing the plan of life; (…) but he has another way to be united to God, and that is through all the suffering that he is going through (…) he offers up his suffering especially "in the heat of the battle", by which he means, when the pain is worse, especially during the night-time (he sleeps very poorly). He is also privileged in that he has time to prepare; he can offer his suffering for the salvation of souls who die unprepared."*

In fact, when he was transferred to the Pain Control Unit, it took several weeks to lessen his pain. Many treatments were tried, but none seemed to solve the problem. As a last resort, it was decided to implant a pump that would supply morphine almost constantly. Soon Pedro's eyes began to cascade with tears. Everyone believed that he was crying from the pain and that the treatment had not worked.

"No. It's not that," he replied. *"It's just that this is the first time in many months that I feel no pain."*

The doctor later confessed to his parents that alleviating Pedro's pain had been one of the greatest challenges of his career.

What also made him suffer at times was the attention he received. Pedro *resented being a bother.* He preferred to try to do himself everything he could do on his own. But at times he became frustrated with his limitations and tears came to his eyes. It was very tough for him to realise that he could do less and less and had to ask more and more for help. As he lost his abilities in the final few weeks, he had a hard time having to accept help even for very basic needs. But he learned to be humble and to obey in that as well. As Chema put it: *"he was willing to trust whatever the directors asked of him, seeing behind it the Will of God."*

Despite the pain he was in, Pedro did not slacken in his plan of mortifications and sacrifices. Anyone could have thought, "With all that he has already gone through, why is he looking for new mortifications?" Well, to be holy, to become a saint. He wrote in his diary: *"Offer more mortifications. For my sins and for the dead."* Pedro continued to practise mortifications as if he were healthy. During his illness he continued to shower with cold water, abstaining from meat on Fridays, practising little mortifications at meals, in resting, in screen time...

Among the things he found difficult to offer was what St. Josemaría called the *heroic minute* at night and in the morning: going to bed and getting up at a fixed time. In many of his notes he repeats the resolution of going to bed immediately after the examination of conscience. This point, in theory so simple, he found especially difficult. There, already sitting on his bed, he could entertain himself by answering messages or reading emails that came to him, or by checking the news. He never stopped fighting on this point because many things depended on it, as this note shows: *"Fight harder to do the norms well. For this, get to bed quickly."* He knew well that a tired soldier can't fight properly.

In April 2016 he did his spiritual retreat. He took many notes which have been kept. On the second day he wrote: *"Death is life. I have to love all souls. We don't know when we're going to die, but there's a lot to do."* He used death therefore as an incentive: *"Think of death to help me take off again: Would God be happy if He had to judge me today?"*

Pedro lived the virtue of temperance conscientiously, as reflected in his personal notes. He was partly forced to do so by illness; he had to give up some of his favourite foods for health reasons. In particular, he was crazy about Jaffa cakes. He joked saying that temperance, for him, was to eat only *"one packet of Jaffa cakes."* He always ate what he was given, although nausea caused by the treatment sometimes prevented him from doing so.

Although he liked whisky, and was given bottles as gifts from time to time, he tried to serve it personally to others and often didn't even try it himself. In general, he preferred non-alcoholic drinks.

"After evening Mass," Greygarth's diary reads, *"he stayed to have a little of what was on offer, just the tomato juice. The juice was spicy, and he winced on tasting it, but he soldiered on and finished the glass. (...) He explained that owing to the chemotherapy, the inside of his mouth is so sore (...) that he can take only fluids at the moment."*

He fought seriously to practise temperance, not only in relation to food, but especially when using the computer and the iPad, watching YouTube videos (above all, on the Middle East conflict and some political news items), and not giving in to distractions when studying or working, or when doing his prayer. During his examination of conscience at night, he noted many times the interior mortification of fighting to control his imagination, especially when in bed waiting to fall asleep.

"To follow Christ means to deny oneself," he wrote one day. *"Do not seek the easy way. But don't worry: it won't always be that hard."*

The virtue of humility is a gift and also a conquest. Often Pedro was helped by his mother or father; at other times by Patricio, who was a doctor. On one occasion Patricio asked Javier to help Pedro to go to the toilet, because he wanted him to learn so that he could give Pedro's mother some rest. Seeing his mother there, Pedro became angry: *"My mum is out there; why doesn't she do it?"*

Javier told him that the doctor wanted others to learn as well for when his mother wasn't there. When Pedro heard that, he lowered his gaze. He was silent for a few seconds, took a deep breath and explained to Javier what he had to do. He never complained again about being helped. But it was apparent how much it cost him to be so vulnerable, unable even to clean himself after going to the toilet.

In his prayer he often asked for the virtue of humility. Most of the time he simply wrote the word, *"Humility"* in his examination. Or he referred to his lack of humility: *"Be more humble. I get angry because I'm proud."* And he referred to his anger: *"I'm getting more annoyed at people: I've been angry with the Spanish lads and with my brothers."*

He prayed for humility to have the courage to correct other numeraries, so that the comments of others, be they good or bad, would not affect him. *"No getting discouraged: More humility!"* he wrote one day. A soul that fights keeps track of both victories and defeats: *"I have criticised someone else's driving and was a sore loser after a chess game,"* he noted another day in his examination, to remember when preparing his confession.

On another occasion he got angry with someone who was working on his doctoral thesis. When that person came to visit him one day, Pedro reminded him that he had to write his thesis and that he should not be wasting time while he was with him. It hurt him to see himself as a burden to others. After that day, those who came from Greygarth to accompany him did not forget to bring a book with them.

When the pain was such that he could not sleep, he noticed it much more when he woke up. These were the hardest struggles of his *"mental battle"* and sometimes he had anxiety attacks. He had not suffered from these before his illness and they only happened occasionally in his last months. When they occurred, he would go to his room for a few minutes to rest and come back later as if nothing had happened.

The enemy never gives up. Until the last moment, he tries to snatch souls from God. Among the battles to be fought as the end approaches is faith. Faith that God is there. Faith that what happens makes some sense. Until the end, the enemy never gives up a soul for lost and he knows how to torment his victims. There were times when everything went well. When in October 2016 the pain was more under control, he wrote in his prayer: *"I don't have any test of faith troubling me. Life is easy."* This lasted just a few weeks, because soon the enemy came to do battle with him.

When towards the end of his illness Pedro had a really hard time sleeping, temptations would come, some of them strong temptations against hope: *"What if I don't go to Heaven?"* he sometimes commented to those in whom he could confide most deeply. One of those nights he woke up Andy, who was sleeping next to him, and said, *"I wonder how Montse Grases[1] managed when she saw that she was dying."* This kind of thought often comes when death is approaching and is an opportunity to abandon oneself with confidence in divine mercy. It is good to remember that Heaven is always a gift.

On other occasions, awake at midnight, he was attacked by the enemy with temptations against holy purity. Regarding these, he noted in his examination: *"Go to Our Lady. Get up when the battle gets harder."*

It also caused him suffering to realise that, with the pain, he had become more impatient with others and he was finding it more and more difficult to smile. It was also difficult for him physically because in his last month he had mouth sores that hurt when he smiled.

Someone commented one day to Pedro that he always looked cheerful. Pedro corrected him immediately and told him that this wasn't true,

---

1. Venerable Montserrat Grases García (10 July 1941 – 26 March 1959) was a Spanish member of Opus Dei who died in similar conditions. Cheerful and pious, compassionate towards the poor and the ill, she was also diagnosed with bone cancer continuing to demonstrate a cheerful demeanour centred on offering her suffering to God. The cause for her beatification was opened after her death in 1962.

it was because he saw him with good eyes. He explained that there were times when he had a really hard time keeping cheerful, but he knew it was his personal battle and that others didn't have to *suffer it*.

He also felt frustrated when finding he was falling asleep during prayer or in thanksgiving after Communion; or when, in his last weeks, he would fall asleep while he was talking to someone. He suffered because, due to the medication, he could not pray well or pay attention to God or to others.

The centre of his plan of life continued to be the Eucharist and his devotion was evident. Archbishop Roche said that one day he went to celebrate Mass for the family and was surprised that Pedro was on his knees during the entire Eucharistic prayer. At the end, Pedro said to him: "*I would have liked it to go on a little longer.*" And that evening, the Cardinal wrote to a friend: "*There is a mystical quality about him... All I am certain of is that he is serene and not at all self-conscious or self-absorbed – such effortless beauty. This is an extraordinary grace...*"

Evidently, there were many days when it was not possible for him to attend Holy Mass or to pray in front of a tabernacle. However, he managed to receive Communion almost every day. But sometimes, due to nausea, he couldn't. To be able to attend Mass, the schedule of Masses in Greygarth was modified, or the Mass was said in his room. When that was not possible, Communion was brought to him by the priest. Pedro never ceased to thank everyone for the effort they made to enable him to attend Mass or receive Communion.

Ever since he had got used to visiting Jesus in the tabernacle at his school in Mallorca, he kept trying to make a visit every day. Later, when he was already living with the Blessed Sacrament in the same house, he tried not to get used to it and go to the oratory many times. As he said one day to another, "*May I never get used to having God at home.*"

In August 2016, when speaking with his spiritual director, they decided that for a time Pedro would try to make more visits to the Blessed Sacrament in the oratory. Being physically limited, Pedro noticed that he had reduced the number of visits. The following week, taking stock, he said: "*I have made many more visits to the Blessed Sacrament this week.*" Holiness is the struggle for love. There is nothing more to it.

The last time he managed to go down to the oratory he had to make an enormous effort, in the midst of his pain, and with the help of several others. He wanted to go to see our Lord, "*to return the visit*", since He came to see him in his room every day.

The fact that Mass was at the centre of his spiritual

life was also conveyed in the way he encouraged everyone to attend. When he was already very ill, and his mother wanted to be with him as long as possible, Pedro asked her to go to Mass and asked her not to return until she had finished her thanksgiving.

When he could only receive Communion outside of Mass, he requested it daily and received it with great devotion. Even when he could not speak because of the sores that the chemotherapy left in his mouth, he always said the responses of the Communion rite. And when he could no longer swallow well, he was given a small part of the Consecrated Host, or even a few drops of the Precious Blood.

One day, Fr Sean brought him Communion, but he did not find a suitable table to act as an altar on which to rest the pyx – the silver box containing Hosts to take to the sick. The priest decided to place the pyx on Pedro's chest, as he was lying on the bed. Pedro was very moved by this and his voice failed when Fr Sean explained that he was the best altar in that room.

Sometimes it was difficult for him to go to confession frequently. Although his plan was to go weekly, sometimes he forgot. In one of his notes he wrote: *"need to go to our Lord all the time for healing. Schedule a day every week for confession. Weekly confession is part of our plan of life."* He didn't fail to jot it down when he failed: *"Confession:*

more than two weeks!" And on another day he wrote: *"Prepare confession better. Get to confession every Saturday."*

As the days were pretty chaotic, sometimes he left some of the norms of his plan of life till very late. Sometimes he was seen reading the gospel after the exam. Or he noted that he had forgotten to pray the *Angelus* or meditate on the mysteries of the rosary. On the most difficult days, he really found it hard. In August 2017 he wrote in his notes: *"Apathy for doing the norms. I forget or I just don't want to do them when it's time."*

In those last months, his plan of life had to be adapted to his circumstances. Still, he would try to demand more of himself. On August 16 2017 he wrote: *"You can do more of the plan of life."* True: he failed. But he never stopped trying.

Pedro had a great love for Our Lady. In addition to praying the rosary daily and various other prayers throughout the day, he always wore the scapular of Our Lady of Mount Carmel around his neck. Every October, a Marian procession was organised in St Edward's parish. Pedro continued to go during the three years of his illness, with increasing difficulty. He was responsible for getting volunteers and was part of the organising committee and for the procession on October 1, 2016. The following year, on October 7, 2017, although he could no longer walk, he did not want to miss it and went by car instead.

During his final months he was aware that, while saying the Rosary or doing the gospel reading or the prayer, he would become tremendously sleepy. But he always tried to keep awake. He didn't give up. As he mentioned to some friends who were with him in hospital, prayer had become a real *challenge* for him in his situation. It is something that appears often in the notes of his examination of conscience: *"Pay more attention in the prayer."*

Sometimes, in between so many visits, he lost track of the time and night would fall before he had finished his prayer, his ten minutes of spiritual reading or the rosary. He needed help, and he asked for it, so that he would not neglect those times of conversation that he had with God.

Another prayer he said every day was the *Preces*; a set of prayers brought together by St. Josemaría, drawn from prayers and texts of Sacred Scripture and the liturgy and said in Latin by the members of Opus Dei. One day in Lent Pedro wrote in his notes: *"The Preces. Lent is a time of prayer. I should try to pray the Preces better. They unite me to all the members of Opus Dei in the world. Serviam! That is what my whole vocation consists of: Service."*

Of his personal prayer there are few notes. Sometimes he took notes that later served to give circles to the students. One of those days he wrote, *"No one seems to know who Jesus is. However, he has fulfilled all the Messianic prophesies: Son of David and* *from Bethlehem. We are lucky enough to know who Jesus is and what He has done for us. We should tell our friends that Jesus is the Son of God and that He came down to die for us. Many people may **know** this but probably don't fully **understand** its significance."*

As his illness got worse, his plan of life became erratic. His prayer ended up divided into several parts, he found it very difficult to do his spiritual reading and on some days he could not visit Jesus in the tabernacle. When he expressed his concern about this, the priest explained that the plan of life is a means, not an end. The goal is to be a contemplative soul, to speak with God at all times. One can be united to God by doing mental prayer or simply by going up to Calvary accompanying Jesus and letting oneself be accompanied by Him.

"In that case my plan of life lasts 24 hours a day," he replied. And so it did.

His mother realised that when Pedro felt really ill, he didn't usually tell anyone. One day she protested and she told him that if he didn't feel well, he should say so. He ought to let her know... and God too. Pedro smiled at her and said, *"Don't worry mum, I'm talking to Him all the time."*

Something that made Pedro suffer was not being able to see the apostolic fruits of all this. Many times, to encourage him, people told him how fruitful his sacrifice was. They told him of souls in one place or another who were getting closer to God. He would smile, but said to those closest to him, *"Yes. That's all well and good. But I don't see anything."*

Perhaps God decided to keep him unaware of all that so as to help him to be humble because, in fact, hundreds of souls came closer to God thanks to Pedro's prayer and example.

Sometimes, when someone told him that his suffering would lead to a springtime of vocations, he felt even more frustrated because he would never see all that flowering which, in faith, he trusted that God would send later. *"Yes. I'm sure it will come,"* he said with resignation, *"when I am no longer here. Like Moses, I will miss out on all the good things."*

Young vocations began to come. One day, when he was showing his fish tank to Peter, one of the directors passed by. Pedro said he wanted to talk to him. After Peter had left, Pedro burst into tears saying to the director, *"I won't see it. Everything will come about when I am gone."*

The truth is that God did allow him to see some of the fruit, but the enemy did not give him any respite. Let us not forget that discouragement is the greatest weapon of the enemy. Sometimes Pedro expected much more or became impatient with souls who simply did not respond.

One day his brother Javier, with tears in his eyes, told him that it was not fair that it was he, Pedro, who had to go through all that. Why did God repay his generosity with so much suffering and an early death? Pedro understood his brother's suffering. He hugged him and said:

"After all I have seen in these three years, after so many conversions and having brought so many closer to God, I would go through all this again without a second thought. It's worth it!"

When he received visitors he tried to pay attention, listen, encourage and smile. But all this required so much effort that, when left alone with his parents, brothers or the members of the Work, he would fall asleep. With them he could rest. To them he opened his heart, in them he found support and from them received comfort.

He suffered and cried. He cried sometimes through physical suffering, in silence. He cried at times also because of the darkness he felt, because of the goodbyes, because he was running out of time to be with the people he loved, because he saw those who were with him suffer. He cried. One day, his dad saw him in tears; when he asked Pedro what was wrong, Pedro lifted his gaze and said: *"Dad, I just love everything!"*

Oh, yes. He cried at times during those last weeks of his life. But then he calmly tried to leave everything in God's hands, again and again, some days dozens of times. And then he devoted himself to those who came to see him without them noticing his inner suffering.

Fr Sean Riley, a diocesan priest who went to see him, said as he left his room that he was bowled over by his conversation, bearing in mind what was looming in the background; he simply had not expected him to be *"so serene and entertaining and infectiously happy all at once."*

A couple of weeks before he died, Javier was spending the night by his side. At midnight Pedro asked for help to go to the bathroom. There were moments when he was more wakeful and you could talk to him a little more. With a lot of effort, he managed to sit up. As he took a breath he said, *"How much longer do I have to carry on with all this?"*

Javier told him that it was until God wanted and tried to comfort him, reminding him that we were all very grateful that he was still with us. Pedro was silent and after a while went to bed peacefully. As you can see, his serenity was not the result of not having sufferings or not fully realising his situation. His peace came from a conscious abandonment into the hands of God that he had to constantly renew.

12. Faithful until death

In August 2017 he managed to spend a few weeks on a course in Holland with a group of young numeraries from many different countries. There he had the opportunity to see the prelate of Opus Dei in person for the last time. In his eagerness to keep improving, he continued to write down resolutions on his phone. The day after joining the annual course he wrote in his prayer:

"Put order in your day. Learn the names of each one. Talk to each of them. Humility. Fraternal corrections, do it for them. Think of the apostolate for the coming year."

Due to the pain, he was unable to finish the course and had to return to Manchester two days early. His leg was very swollen and it was already difficult for him to move. He needed help going to the bathroom, getting up, and getting dressed.

He was given a room in Greygarth that was easier to access and was large enough to house all the equipment he needed. His parents and brothers came to see him there every day.

The pain was getting more and more intense. His right leg swelled and he could no longer support weight on it. The tumour began to compress other internal organs and the discomfort multiplied. By October the cancer had metastasised and reached his lungs.

In the autumn of 2017, Pedro was heading into the final stretch. The doctors communicated that they had exhausted all resources and from then on they would only administer palliative treatment. As he had only a few months left to live, he was asked if he preferred to die in hospital or at home. He asked to go home, but to the surprise of the doctors, he explained that home was not his parents' house, but Greygarth. Doctors couldn't get the idea that he wanted to die in a students' residence when his parents lived just 15 minutes away. But his parents confirmed his decision.

Although also both members of the Work, they offered him the possibility of dying at home. It would be less hassle for those who lived in Greygarth, with daily visits from doctors, nurses, families and friends... After all, his father was a doctor and, moreover, who can take better care of a sick person than his own mother?

But Pedro told several people on different occasions that his home and family was Opus Dei, *"My brothers need me and I need my brothers."*

From then on the farewells began.

Since Pedro loved unreservedly and was loved so much, saying goodbye to him was hard for everyone. When we realised that the final opportunities to talk to him were approaching, many of us went to see him. He wanted us all to come to his room and have some time alone with him so he could talk to each one personally for the last time.

He received thousands of visits before he died. Some days about a hundred people came to see him. One day he was upset to discover that some people had left without seeing him because, with the morphine and sleepless nights, he was asleep when they came. That is why he always asked to be woken up and told his parents:

"Do not allow any visitor to leave without seeing me, at least for a minute. Don't send anyone away."

Javier, who was returning to Guatemala, went to say goodbye on December 31. Finding Pedro asleep, he woke him up as requested. As soon as Pedro opened his eyes, Javier said, *"Pedro, I'm leaving."* Pedro smiled and they melted into an embrace of tears. Pedro said to him, *"Forgive me. Forgive me because I have given you a lot of work... you have had to help me in so many things!"*

Surprised, Javier apologised for not having known how to help him more and better. Then Pedro thanked him for having lived in Greygarth during those months and being there with them.

This kind of exchange was repeated countless times with many of us in various ways.

The pain began to be constant and acute, his nights long and his urgency to prepare well, more pressing. He told the priest that when the pain was most intense, usually in the middle of the night, he repeated the names of those who had asked him for prayers.

He also said that he considered himself fortunate, privileged to be able to prepare to die, something that many did not have, and that is why he offered his sufferings for those who died without being ready for death.

Managing to calm the pain was an odyssey, but Pedro kept smiling as long as he could and receiving whoever wanted to come and see him. When he was not sleepy from the effect of medication and sleepless nights, Pedro spoke normally and continued to take an interest in everyone. For example, he kept a bottle of whisky for Fr Robert in case he came to see him, knowing how much this Scottish priest liked it.

Nor did the pain make him lose his sense of humour. Talking to Fr Andrew about his funeral, they discussed what language it should be in. Pedro commented that many Spaniards would surely come and most of them would not understand English very well. So, he suggested with a smile that it would be best for the funeral to be *"in English with Spanish subtitles."*

During those last months of 2017 Pedro went into hospital several times for a few days to receive treatment. On one of those days, his brother Carlos asked him to pray for a friend of his whom he had been trying to convince to go to confession for a long time. Pedro assured him that he would pray and asked him to introduce his friend to him. Carlos brought his friend to Pedro's room and after a five-minute conversation, the fellow said he wanted to talk to a priest.

Pedro was well aware that he was dying and that, from that time onwards he would be doing many things for the last time. On Sunday, November 19, there was a celebration for his father's birthday. Many family members had come from Spain for the occasion, and with the intention of seeing Pedro. At one point, surrounded by everyone, Pedro couldn't contain himself and began to cry. He knew it was the last time he would celebrate his father's birthday on earth.

In early December Pedro left the hospital and returned to Greygarth. There he was accompanied at all hours of the day and night. His parents were there all day, every day. With his wheelchair he could still go out to eat from time to time with family or friends and enjoyed it. And, when his health permitted, he ate with the residents in the dining room and went to the get-together with everyone.

Each morning two nurses came to visit him. On the first day both of them were Catholic. They were very impressed. After all, they came to visit a patient who wanted to die in a students' residence and that was very difficult for them to understand.

Pedro's mother showed them round Greygarth. In particular she took them to see the oratory and explained everything she could. They were so impressed that word began to spread through the hospital. Many nurses who came already expected to see *"something surprising that they would never have seen before."*

Sometimes doctors and nurses came outside of their working hours, as did his GP, to help in any way they could. There were days when up to four nurses came from the hospital; a figure somewhat disproportionate, explained perhaps by their desire to see the place.

On December 19, he was diagnosed with an infection and returned to hospital. There he was given oxygen. At one point on the next morning when he was finding it difficult to breathe, he turned to Andy and his brother Carlos and said, as if cheering up: *"There is little left."* He smiled at them and said *"Thank you for being around."* Realising he was getting emotional, and faithful to his character, he added: *"But don't get sentimental now, huh?"*

As already explained, Pedro did not particularly like very emotional manifestations of affection. Weak though he was, he still tried to dodge kisses from his father or withdrew his hand when his mother tried to take his between her own. Perhaps this came from his years in Yorkshire, where he grew up.

The cancer had already invaded almost the whole of his lungs and Pedro needed oxygen when breathing became a struggle. As soon as he got his rhythm back a little, he began to welcome visitors very affectionately to such an extent that many did not notice his difficulty breathing. At one point there were more than a dozen people in his hospital room.

Three days later, on December 22, Pedro said goodbye to the hospital patients and doctors and returned to Greygarth to die at home. There he was received by the residents with joy and had a brief get-together with them. Pedro even felt strong enough to watch a film and have pizza with them (although he no longer ate it).

December was the month of farewells when many of us saw him for the last time. Pedro always received and spoke to each one on his own. Tom, a young numerary, also talked with him. At one point, Pedro asked him if he was happy with his vocation. Tom said yes, and simply asked Pedro the same question.

"I've never been happier," replied Pedro with a smile.

During those final days Pedro repeated to many of us on numerous occasions that the last three years had been the happiest of his life.

As soon as the residents left for the Christmas holidays, some rooms were set aside so that his brothers Carlos and Javi could be close to him at all hours. His parents would also spend the whole day at Greygarth and often the night as well. Domestic staff worked overtime to ensure that the family never lacked anything. They even went so far as to help his parents with their Christmas shopping so that they could be with Pedro.

After the oratory, Pedro's room had become the busiest and most important one in the house. Christmas Eve was spent singing carols there with Pedro. The next day, December 25, everyone followed Pope Francis' Urbi et Orbi blessing. Then Fr Joe celebrated Christmas Mass in the same room with Pedro and his family.

That afternoon Santa Claus came to bring his gifts to Pedro's room, where everyone was crammed together like sardines. They celebrated in a big way. They also had time to watch the Queen's speech and ended up watching a film.

Every day he received Holy Communion. If he could not attend Mass, the priest brought him Holy Communion in the pyx. The table in his room acted as an altar. The Host was placed there with candles and Pedro made the visit, then spent 10 minutes in adoration and finally received Holy Communion from the priest.

On New Year's Eve they had Mass in his room and again a celebration afterwards. At midnight they took the opportunity to send a video to the prelate of Opus Dei through Don Mariano Fazio, in which Pedro wished him a Happy New Year. It did not take long for a message from the Father to arrive in response, sending his blessing to Pedro and those who were with him.

The following days were quieter. The visits continued. One of them was from Michael, a podiatrist who took advantage of his visit to cut Pedro's toenails and bandage one that was bleeding. As Pedro's leg was now enormous, Michael began to roll the bandage up around his foot. Gradually, to tighten it he had to stretch his arms wide, making circles around the bed, taking steps backwards. Pedro was amused and he explained that it made him anxious because it seemed to him that poor Michael was going along the corridors holding the end of his bandage.

On the first day of the year 2018 Pedro had the joy of welcoming Our Lord in the monstrance. There was a period of adoration in the room, with all the Greygarth residents packed in. It ended with the blessing and at the end Pedro received Holy Communion.

"There's no better way to start the year," he said with a smile.

Some days he still managed to go down to eat with everyone in the dining room. The visits continued. Among others, a nurse came to visit him, not as a nurse anymore, she explained, but *"as a family friend"*. There she explained to those present that when Pedro told her he wanted to go to Greygarth to die, she tried to dissuade him by saying that he should go to his parents' house, where they would take much better care of him. But now that she had seen Greygarth, the people living there and the atmosphere of the house, now that she had seen what happened within those walls, she realised how wrong she was. She concluded: *"How I would like to be part of this family!"*

As of January 9, Pedro began spending most of the day unconscious. From time to time he would open his eyes and ask for something. That day Fr Gerry celebrated Mass in his room and was able to give him Communion, a few drops of Precious Blood from the Chalice. As it was St. Josemaría's birthday, he was brought a relic of the saint for him to kiss.

By Thursday, January 11, Pedro was barely moving or opening his eyes. At one point, his mother came close to him to adjust the oxygen tube. Without opening his eyes and with great effort, Pedro put his arms around her and embraced her for the last time. He used up all the energy he had left to give his mum a strong hug. After that he didn't move any more.

The next day they received a call from Don Carlos Nannei, an Argentine priest and friend of Pope Francis. The Pope had asked him to call Pedro and his family to tell them that he remembered the visit they had made to him and was praying for them and thanked Pedro for his prayers, since in various ways Pedro had sent him the message that he offered his sufferings for the Pope. Pope Francis sent him his apostolic blessing.

On 12 January the visits continued. Many came to pray, but Pedro no longer opened his eyes. Over the course of the whole day he only managed to eat a tangerine and drink a few sips of water from his mother's hand. His grandmother Rosario and a couple of his uncles arrived in Manchester that night.

Arriving at his room already in the early hours of Saturday, January 13, they found that there was a crowd praying very peacefully. They were saying the rosary and when it finished, several of them began to pray the *Salve Regina* in Spanish. Just as they uttered the words, *"Turn then most gracious advocate thine eyes of mercy towards us,"* at twenty-eight minutes past one, Pedro gave up his soul.

As one of his uncles explained, *"Had I been offered the choice of being present at some event on this earth, this would be the one I would choose."*

13. From Heaven

Fr Michael celebrated the first Mass right there in the room, still crowded.

Among the women numeraries of Opus Dei in Manchester there was a nurse. Guided by her, several women of the Work helped Pedro's mother to prepare Pedro's body and place it in the oratory. Pedro had now become patrimony of the whole Work.

Hundreds of people went to pray and several priests celebrated Holy Mass before his mortal remains in the oratory of Greygarth. Soon messages began to arrive from all over the world. Among the first, a message from the Father, who wrote from Rome:

I have just received the news that Pedrito has gone from us to Heaven this morning and I am praying for him closely united to you. The Blessed Virgin, whom he loved so much – he gave me a beautiful statue of hers when I was in London – has taken him by the hand on a Saturday. Let us thank her for this motherly gesture, which is a consolation for us in the midst of grief.

Last summer, I had the opportunity to have a chat while with Pedrito in Holland. He has been a man especially mature for his age, and Our Lord has given him numerous graces to which he has responded generously: thus, he has faced illness with joy, giving those who accompanied the present of his smile, supernatural outlook, giving suffering and life an apostolic meaning... Gifts that he received from God and that he shared with everyone. Now, from Heaven, he will be seeing with total clarity what he has sown, and the fruit of his self surrender projected in time, in Manchester and in the whole world.

Convey to my sons in Greygarth my deep gratitude for the way they have cared for him during these years, together with his parents and brothers. It gave me great joy to speak with Esperanza and Pedro by video, from London; I join them in their sorrow and pray that it will be transformed into serenity and peace, thinking of the complete happiness that their son enjoys.

I send you my most affectionate blessing, with the wonderful memory of my recent stay among you.

Your Father,
Fernando

Literally thousands of messages came from people whose lives had changed thanks to Pedro. Sick people whom he had helped, friends, school friends and university classmates, priests, bishops and archbishops.

Some had known him for only a few months. Like those three months he spent at Imperial College. One of his companions said: *"Pedro is the happiest person I have ever met in my life."* Another said that Pedro had been an inspiration to him even before his illness, but much more so during the last years. Another said that Pedro had been the most considerate, faithful, understanding, and positive person he had ever met in his life. There were hundreds of testimonies of this kind.

Practically all the messages referred to Pedro's smile, his joy, good humour and always encouraging and positive comments. One boy commented that he had had conversations with Pedro about the existence of God in which he had declared himself an agnostic. When the news of Pedro's death reached him, he explained: *"I began to talk to him, with the certainty that he was listening to me. I think that's praying. Today I have begun to pray again."*

Several spoke of his ability to make people feel important, his attentiveness to everything he was told, his ability to listen and understand. *"Pedro always made me feel special. It didn't matter if there were a lot of people there. When he talked to me, he talked as if he was alone with me."*

There were testimonies of people who had come back to religious practice. A cancer patient whom he met in hospital spoke to the chaplain of Greygarth and let him know that he wanted to be baptised. Most of the messages assumed that Pedro was already in heaven and that rather than praying for him, they entrusted petitions to him.

On January 23, the funeral took place at the *Holy Name Church* in Manchester. The Mass was celebrated by archbishop Arthur Roche with more than 30 priests concelebrating and the church was crowded. There present were his family, members of Opus Dei, classmates from school and university, friends. There were very many young people there. It was especially moving to see doctors and nurses from the hospital attend the funeral in their white coats, taking a break from their day's work so as not to miss that moment. Students at his university who had known him or seen him on campus attended, as well as other cancer patients, some in wheelchairs.

One of the funeral directors could not believe what he was seeing and wanted to know everything about Pedro. The person responsible for preparing Pedro's body went to see his mother to tell her how deeply impressed everyone had been on seeing Pedro. On the one hand, he could see the swollen leg; the tumour was clearly evident. He said he could imagine the pain Pedro must have suffered, and yet his calm face looked as if it was a different person.

A lady explained how she had gone to Mass at the Holy Name Church and found herself at the funeral. She saw a priest appear, followed by...

30 more priests and finally an archbishop, from Rome. Hundreds of people. And she began to wonder who that boy was. How can a 21-year-old boy attract so many people to his funeral? So she asked who this Pedro was – and then understood. She concluded by saying, *"I will never forget this day."*

After the church funeral came the journey to the cemetery. The driver of the funeral car taking Pedro's brothers and archbishop Roche to the cemetery heard them pray the rosary in the back seat. When they got out at the cemetery, the driver came over to ask the archbishop what they were doing during the trip. He explained that they were saying the rosary and that man, who was not a Christian, said: *"In all my years working in funeral homes I have never experienced so much peace. It's the most beautiful funeral I've ever seen in my life."*

At the end of the burial a member of Opus Dei went to thank one of the funeral director's staff. He saw that the employee was not going away and he felt he ought to tell him that he could leave now because the ceremony was over. The man's reply was simply, *"Yes, I know. I'm praying."*

Priests who knew Pedro were grateful to have met him. Fr Chris remembered how Pedro and his brothers served Mass and would run to be the first to blow out the candles at the end of Sunday Mass. He remarked, *"Seeing Pedro grow* into such an impressive and remarkable young man has been one of the greatest blessings of my life," and he expressed perfectly the thoughts of many of us, priests, adding: "*Pedro had a wonderful way of affirming my priesthood – and encouraging me to live out my vocation more fully! I shall miss his smile, his hugs, his warm friendliness, his lively intelligence, his sense of fun. I have no doubt that he has made me a better priest and a better person, and I will pray that he will continue to do that from heaven.*"

Liam, one of his friends who became a Catholic, also expressed his gratitude for having met Pedro. Pedro accompanied him on his journey to the faith and gave him catechism classes, becoming his sponsor when he was received into the Catholic Church. In his letter, he talks about how friendship with Pedro led him to friendship with God.

Another friend remembers how it was Pedro who once asked him the most important question of his life: "*Have you ever thought about vocation?*" "*I vividly recall when this question was first put to me,*" explains Karl Gustel Wärnberg. "*It was on the tube towards Tooting on our way to Kelston... For Pedro, this vocation came in the form of a Numerary of Opus Dei and having lived with him I can only be in awe of the dedication he put into following this Divine calling. I saw him while he suffered, but I also spent a lot of time with him in moments of joy, study, and work. He took all these roles upon himself with tremendous fervour. This model of Christian life has*

*been an inspiration to me... It was to no small part
through Pedro that I was inspired to seek my vocation
to the priesthood... Once his illness was discovered and
explained to us, one mutual friend of ours turned to
me and said: 'Perhaps he is the only one of us who is
ready to go?'."*

In a very natural way, those who had known him
began to turn to Pedro for help.

Sofía, a 9-year-old girl from Sencelles (Mallorca)
had written a very colourful letter to Pedro months
before, to tell him that she prayed for him. Pedro
had that letter for a while by his hospital bed.
The day Pedro died Sofía got lost. For more than
an hour they were looking for her anxiously all
over the town. Her mother, unable to endure the
anxiety any longer and remembering that Pedro
had passed away that very morning, prayed to
him aloud: *"Pedro, please return my little girl to me
now."* Immediately a car pulled up next to her
and Sofía ran out to hug her mother. A passer-by
had found the girl and they were driving around
looking for someone who might know her.
Needless to say, even the driver of the car cried at
this happy ending.

Another favour benefited the person who had
taken care of Pedro in his last months. Due to
the lack of sleep and the stress of the last hours
of Pedro's life, Patricio, the doctor who looked
after him at home, woke up with an intense
headache. He thought of going to get a pill,

but it occurred to him that, since the pain had somehow been caused by Pedro, he himself had to solve it. Patricio asked Pedro to get rid of that headache and, immediately, the pain completely disappeared.

Iñaki, a resident of Greygarth who had lived with Pedro during those months, confidently went to the centre of Manchester by car knowing that it would not be easy to find a place to park. He assumed that Pedro would come to his aid. However, when he arrived, he found that there was indeed nowhere to park. He asked Pedro to please help him. But he still didn't find a space. He finally gave up. And getting angry with Pedro, he said to him out loud: *"It's clear that you don't want to help* me!" He hadn't finished saying that when a driver honked his horn for Iñaki to move his car because he wanted to get out of his parking space. *"Okay,"* Iñaki smiled, *"So, we're still friends."*

Epilogue

God is the best of *brokers*. He alone knows how to get the most out of our investments.

Pedro's story is not just Pedro's. God knows well how to get the maximum spiritual benefit out of any situation. St. Josemaría explained that, in the early days of Opus Dei, what made him suffer most was not the poverty he experienced, nor the slander and defamation against him. He said that what made him suffer most were the sufferings of his family and those around him.

With a graphic phrase he explained that, in order to sanctify him, God gave blows with the hammer *"one on the nail and a hundred on the horseshoe."* Seeing himself as the nail, he perceived more blows raining on those around him – the horseshoe. This is how God goes about his plans of sanctification. Always as a team. He does not put just one single person to the test. Rather, he sends a series of tests to a group of people. Thus he reaps the fruits of suffering: from the one who suffers illness in his flesh and also from those who suffer because their loved one is ill.

The proportion is equivalent to that of Calvary: One hangs from the wood, but several suffer next to it. God did not want only the suffering of Christ. He also wanted to reap the fruit of Our Lady's suffering, of St. John's, of St. Mary Magdalen's, of Dismas', as well as that of the other women and of the apostles, who followed everything from a distance, but still suffered it all too.

Life is a race. God has asked us to run for Him. But he has not told us how long a distance it is. We do not know if we have to run 20, 40 or 100 miles. Some of us he has made sprinters, others long-distance runners. God knows exactly what we can run and He will never ask us to run more than our legs and heart can bear.

It's an exhausting race. It's meant to be. So it has been for all the saints and there are no exceptions. And while we run we encourage others to run. As you may have seen, it is not the same to go hiking alone, as to go accompanied. With the encouragement and example of others, we reach further.

When we give our life to God we give it, in some way, to others as well. Because in doing what God asks of us, we inspire others to do the same. To say yes to one's vocation is to repeat: *"Be it done to me, and to those around me, according to your word."*

We have already seen that our God is a demanding God. He always asks for everything. God asks us for our money *and* our life. And both money and life must be given entirely. From start to finish. That is why to give one's life is to give one's death as well. To God and to others. Keep running because God needs it. Keep pulling because others need us. Sometimes, when it seemed that Pedro could do no more, you could see he kept on fighting for those around him. Because they had a right to see the battle and, above all, the victory.

It helps a lot to think of the influence our generosity has on the lives of others. As Pedro once told me, "*I can't slow down*," because he knew he wasn't alone in life's journey. He saw that those around him needed to see his struggle. *We* needed him to keep it up. Usually Pedro didn't need to smile. *We* needed him to smile. Many times he didn't need to get up. *We* needed him to keep standing.

But don't think Pedro was an actor. He wasn't. Nor were the saints. They inspire not because they set their minds to it but because they can't help it. Like a city built on a mountain top. You can't hide a lit candle under the bed; it may end up setting fire to the bed and then the whole house – until the light is finally seen from miles away.

Holiness, like faithfulness, is contagious (I wish it were pandemic!). A good life is transmitted by example. When we see that *it's possible*, we understand that *we also can do it – Possumus!*

For centuries it was thought that it was physically

impossible for humans to run a mile in less than 4 minutes. After thousands of years and millions of races, it still seemed impossible. It was called the *4-minute barrier* and some doctors ventured to say that, if anyone tried to break it, his heart would explode.

But on May 6, 1954, a young Oxford medical student, Roger Bannister, managed to run the mile in 3:59 minutes. That was a feat. And what followed was an even greater feat: Australia's John Landy broke that record the following month. The following year three athletes came in under 4 minutes. Since then thousands of athletes have done it.

It all started when someone proved *it could be done*. So it is with holiness. When you see that someone like you succeeds, you realise that *it can be done*. And if *it can be done...* then you can do it too.

When ordinary people do extraordinary things we want to know how they have done them. Because ordinary people always dream of an extraordinary life. Pedro's is the extraordinary life of a very ordinary boy who fought to get to heaven. And that fight did not go unnoticed. Many witnessed it and have shared anecdotes which have been collected in this book.

The aim of this book has not been to canonise Pedro. Only the Church can do that. Rather, it is to share stories that inspire others to take life seriously. Most of Pedro's life was witnessed, like yours and mine, by God alone. These stories demonstrate aspects of his life witnessed by those of us who knew him. But remember, this is just the tip of the iceberg:

"Saints become saints when no one looks at them — except the One who sees everything."

Pedro came up against the Cross at the age of 18. Because of his illness and his long periods of convalescence, it was possible to talk to him many times. One day when the two of us were travelling by car, he opened his heart in a long conversation.

He explained to me that, upon receiving the diagnosis, he interpreted it as a vocation; as a mission. That of saving souls: his and those of many others in the process. If God chose the Cross, it is because there was no other better way to save us.

And so it will always be: there is no other way to save souls than to suffer for them. If there were, God would have taught it to us. Souls are very expensive. And to save souls we have to bleed for them, weep for them and pray for them.

Nothing unites two people more than suffering together. Therefore, going up to Calvary with Christ and suffering with Him unites us to God more than any other form of prayer. The Cross is God's instrument for making saints. With the Cross one gets to Heaven. Without it, it's not possible. But the cross is heavy. That is why Christ himself offers to be our Simon of Cyrene and to carry it uphill with us, up to the summit.

In theology we speak of a *particular judgment* that comes to us when we die. After this judgment we are repaid according to our works in this life and according to the use we have made of God's graces. But at the end of time there will also be a *general judgment* in which the fruits of our life down the ages will be added to our account.

Because, after we die, our actions still have effects: our words, our deeds, souls whom we have helped and who will help others, multiplying down through the centuries the effect of what we did in our time here below. That is why we need a last judgement at the end of time, in which the merits resulting from the continuing effects of our actions *after* our death will be added, when we are no longer there.

God is the best *broker*; He multiplies the effect of his saints.

On witnessing Pedro's death, someone asked me: "Couldn't God have given him a few more years to live? With all that he has done in such a short space of time, didn't God want him to work many more years for His Kingdom?" The truth is: no.

If God knows that Pedro could do in twenty one years what most of us could only achieve in many more years, who am I to correct God?

God knows the length of time needed for each of His sons and daughters to accomplish their mission. And when they leave this earth, their lives continue to bear fruit. As *Gladiator* says, *"What we do in life echoes in eternity."* It has its echo in heaven, yes. And it also has its echo on earth. When we die we leave this world, but we do not leave it the same as we found it.

You and I are called to leave a sustained musical note in history, the echoes of which will continue to be heard and will harmonise with the notes that others will leave. In this way, life is like a round – a divine round where one repeats his melody, then others join with their own and the harmony of the different voices creates an unforgettable effect.

As I draw these lines to a close, I ask God to help us learn from Pedro's example. Jesus is always a good example, but we must not forget that his Mother was Immaculate and his Father, God. That's a doddle, you might say!

When I preach to young people I sense that they want examples closer to home: Saints with WhatsApp and Spotify, with PlayStations and smartphones... saints who parkour and skate, saints who watch TV, football and YouTube, who find it difficult to sit down to study; saints who have to ask forgiveness of those around them, who make mistakes, who take pills for headaches and who have to remember the dates of birthdays ... Saints of flesh and blood, homely saints, real saints, exemplary, close, ordinary, accessible.

If not, they would be like an athlete who wants to help you get in shape and when they explain their plan, you find out that the guy runs 15 miles every morning, does gymnastics afterwards and only drinks fruit smoothies. *"Well, you know what?"* you think, *"If that's the case, I don't want to be fit."* It's too complicated. *"If I have to be like St. Francis of Assisi or St. Lawrence on the gridiron in order to be holy... I'm not interested,"* people may think.

But no. To be holy you have to be normal, and fight. God does very extraordinary things with very ordinary people. Our lives are like the battle between David and Goliath. How can Pedro, being such a normal boy, touch so many souls and change so many lives? By letting God do it.

St. Josemaría wrote: *"On whether you and I behave as God wants, don't forget it, many great things depend"* and many people too.

A person who lived with Pedro in his last years wrote to me: *"Many people depend on us and we cannot let them down. Even more so now, after what we have seen and lived. There are no more excuses.*

Holiness or nothing. I can no longer say: 'I don't know how to do it!'. 'Liar!' *Our Lord can tell me:* 'Of course you know! I've shown you. You've seen it! You've had it right in front of you'."

"*I've got no excuse.*"

Printed in Great Britain
by Amazon